SOCIALISM WITHOUT THE S

SOCIALISM
WITHOUT
THE STATE

Evan Luard

First published 1979 by
THE MACMILLAN PRESS LTD
London and Basingstoke
Associated companies in Delhi
Dublin Hong Kong Johannesburg Lagos
Melbourne New York Singapore Tokyo

Photoset in Great Britain by
Bristol Typesetting Co Ltd, Bristol
Printed in Great Britain
by Billing & Sons Limited,
Guildford, London and Worcester

British Library Cataloguing in Publication Data

Luard, Evan
  Socialism without the state
  1. Socialism
  I. Title
  335   HX44

ISBN 0-333-25598-4
ISBN 0-333-26221-2 Pbk

Contents

The views expressed in this book are those of the author alone, and do not necessarily represent those of H.M. Government

Introduction:
The Debasement of Socialism

Socialists, over the years, have spent much time and labour discussing what they mean by socialism. Many have held that socialism is concerned above all with the public ownership of the means of production, distribution and exchange. Some have said it is 'about equality'. The man in the street has felt, more vaguely, that socialism is rather like communism, only not so much: a kind of mid-point between the systems of the Soviet Union and the US, with more public ownership and more equality than in the US, but less of each than in the Soviet Union.

What is certain is that the meaning attached to the word has changed significantly over the last century or so. What socialism implies above all, in the eyes of many today, is the dominant control, and in many cases the ownership, of the economic resources of a country by the *state*. Socialism now universally means state socialism.

This represents a vast change from the attitudes towards the state and its role held by early socialists. In the late eighteenth and early nineteenth century, the state was generally regarded as an intimidating and hostile force, to be feared and overcome. At that time, in many parts of Europe the state was controlled by a small and all-powerful oligarchy, in many cases by a single autocrat, who ruled usually in arbitrary and repressive style. Even in the few parliamentary systems, as in Britain, the state was controlled by a relatively small propertied class that was not generally considered representative of the population as a whole.

The political goal upheld by many socialists, therefore, was *liberation* from the state and its apparatus of oppression. This idea is seen not only in writers such as Proudhon, Fourier and Bakunin, who were avowed anarchists (who demanded, that is, the abolition of the state in the traditional sense). It is reflected also in many of the writings of those who declared themselves orthodox socialists.

In calling for the abolition of the capitalist system, or of all private property, and their substitution by social ownership, these did not think in terms of state control of the means of production. Such writers as Robert Owen conceived of a co-operative system of production: the ownership of each individual factory or mill by the workers who worked within it. The syndicalist tradition, which became increasingly important in the century which followed, conceived of the control of each industry by the workers within it.

Marx and Engels were ambivalent about the role of the state. They denounced the existing state as a 'committee for the management of the affairs of the bourgeoisie'. They demanded a workers' revolution that was to take over control of the state, and to establish within it a 'dictatorship of the proletariat'. This would use the state as the instrument for the control of the means of production, and for a redistribution of income and wealth in favour of the dispossessed. It would be of uncertain duration. And they foresaw eventually, in the famous words of Engels, the 'withering away' of the state. Thus they shared the distrust of state power expressed by many of their contemporaries, yet recognised that precisely that power might be the instrument for many of the social and political goals which they themselves preached.[1]

But, over the decades that followed, increasingly socialism came to be seen, both by socialists themselves and by their opponents, as aiming at the *extension* of state power. Everywhere social ownership came to be identified with *state* ownership. The prime instrument for achieving socialist aims was to be *nationalisation*: the acquisition of the means of production and exchange by the nation. And when, after 1917, the first fully socialist state came into being, this was the doctrine which it put into effect, more totally and uncompromisingly than had ever previously been seen.

The state was magnified into the centre of all national activity. Never before, even in the most highly organised autocracies of the nineteenth century, was state power raised to such a level as in the Soviet Union, and later in the East European states established on the Soviet model. Not only was government control imposed over every aspect of life and thought. It was taken for granted that the objective of public ownership – which all socialists shared – was to be secured by placing the whole of industry, trade, land and much of agriculture, directly into the hands of the state. No one, either within those states or elsewhere, expressed surprise at this, since this was what socialism was everywhere by this time assumed to mean. Far from securing the abolition of state power, therefore, far from achieving the 'withering away' of the state, socialism brought about the establishment of a state more powerful, more totalitarian, more ubiquitous in its influence and control, than any the world had yet seen: a system in which not only all forms of economic activity, but social services, communications, art, even thought, were placed fully and directly under its all-embracing power.

In the West a similar identification of social ownership with *state* ownership came about. Here too socialism was to be achieved by 'nationalisation'. 'Public' ownership was assumed to mean the ownership and control of industry by the state.

Nor was it only in this sense that the extension of state power was held to be essential to achieving socialist aims. Already, from the end of the nineteenth century onwards, and not only in socialist states, the state increasingly came to be seen as the natural instrument for the redistribution of wealth and welfare. On the one hand, it could secure a greater degree of equality through the tax system at its disposal. On the other, it could organise social services, old age pensions, a free health service, welfare benefits, public housing, regional policies, and many other similar services to secure a more just distribution of good things within society. So, for this reason too, socialism seemed to require an extension of the role of the state throughout society. Socialists therefore were for 'public', that is, for state, expenditure – expenditure in the interests of the public, the great mass of the people, on whose behalf socialists claimed to be concerned.

The belief in the state as the agent of redistribution and the repository of common ownership was a fully logical position. It was logical because the state seemed the only available source of power by which such changes could be brought about. It was only through the tax system and social services, which the state controlled, that redistribution could be achieved. It was only through state control of industry and other economic resources that the goal of public ownership of assets previously in private hands could be attained. So it was no matter for surprise that increasingly the idea of socialism came everywhere to be identified with the expansion and strengthening of state power.

And yet that identification undoubtedly represents a paradox. This is not only because it contrasts with the distrust and fear of the state and its power expressed by many early socialists. For it was not altogether impossible that the *character* of the state might have

changed: from being a tyrannical to being a benevolent force.
According to such a view the essential and all-important difference
was between a state controlled by the bourgeoisie, and used in their
interests, and one controlled by the propertyless, and used in the
interests of all.

Yet even on this ground, it is at least open to question whether
the modern state, yet more powerful and more all-pervasive than
its predecessor a century ago, must necessarily, because of the
change in the forces controlling it, become less oppressive;
whether, simply because once every few years its subjects may today
have the right to choose between one set of leaders and another, the
overwhelming concentration of power in the state's hands becomes
significantly less frightening than the concentration of power in
autocratic or bourgeois states a century and a half ago; whether,
even if it is (in some cases) 'democratically' controlled, it necessarily represents the ideal agent for social ownership. It would be at
least open to argument that, in the eyes of each individual
inhabitant, the modern state was equally remote, equally unpredictable and arbitrary in its commands, equally unacceptable in
the constraints it imposed compared with its predecessor a century
or so ago, irrespective of the constitutional system which may exist
within it.

But even leaving aside this argument, even assuming that a
democratically controlled state, ultimately responsible to the mass
of its inhabitants, is different in kind from the autocratic and
oligarchic states which inspired such fear in earlier times, the
paradox remains. For it still leaves the question: is the ideal of
social ownership, as demanded by the early socialists, and by many
today, in fact adequately fulfilled by state ownership and state
control as practised in socialist states today? This immediately
raises a question which is at the core of socialist thought (a core that
is none the less often avoided in much modern political discussion): what is social ownership, and what do we demand from it?

If social ownership is interpreted merely as a form of ownership
that is 'public' in the formal sense, which is not in private hands,
not based on a competitive system of economic organisation, which
offers no wasteful rewards to unproductive shareholders, then state
ownership might perhaps be held to represent the most appropriate system, at least for certain industries. It could be maintained
that in modern conditions, industries such as the railways,
coalmining, electricity, gas and airlines are *natural* monopolies;

that there is no place for competition there; and that in these circumstances they are better run as state monopolies, in the interests of all, than as private monopolies, whose owners would secure unjustifiable windfall gains as a result of their monopoly situation.

This argument, however, begs the question we are here concerned with. For it assumes that, where industries should be public monopolies, they must be state monopolies. Even if it is accepted (as it must be) that there are good grounds for such industries being run as public industries (since there is no room in them for competition), there is no automatic reason why they should be run at the level of the *state*. But all are conditioned by the concentration of power in the state which has already taken place to the automatic assumption that public ownership and control must mean state ownership and control. Yet there is no automatic reason on grounds of efficiency why railways should not be organised at the continental (say the European) level, electricity at the regional, or coalmines at the area level. And this applies even more to industries such as steel, aircraft, the ports and many others where there is no natural presumption in favour of monopoly at all.

But to use this argument is in fact to use the arguments of capitalism: that the main criterion for deciding such matters must be economic efficiency alone. Yet we may believe in social ownership, like many early socialists, on quite other grounds. We may desire it because we believe it is in the interests of those who work in the enterprise or industry concerned. The arguments used by Marx and others about the 'alienation' of the worker who is obliged to give his labour for the profit of others, who is merely the tool in the hands of the enterpreneur, certainly imply that one of the basic objectives of social ownership should be to give the worker a greater sense of control over his own destiny: a feeling of self-determination, of willing participation in the economic activity in which he is engaged.

But if this is the objective, then the grounds for believing that social ownership must mean state ownership are still more questionable. For it is very difficult to maintain that the alienation of the railwayman in Britain is very much less today because he is working for nationalised British Rail, than it was forty years ago when he worked for the private LNER or LMS. The railwayman's sense of being in control of his own destiny, his sense of participation in the decisions which affect his livelihood, even his sense of 'ownership' of the resources with which he works, is no greater now than it was then. The state, which owns his industry and the tools with which he works, is as remote in his eyes as the directors and shareholders of the old private company which went before. For the fact is that alienation results not merely from the feeling of working for others (and even working for the state may not feel like working for oneself) but, far more, from the *size* of the organisation within which work is undertaken. It is the scale of the enterprise, rather than the system of ownership, the 'production relations', which creates that sentiment. And that scale is no less today than it was yesterday; and it is no less in public industry than it is in private. Indeed in very many industries, whether private or public, the scale is now infinitely greater than before, the controlling authority even more remote, and the sense of alienation therefore more profound than ever.

But another reason for demanding social ownership has been that this is in the interest not merely of the worker in that particular enterprise or industry, but in the interests of every citizen of the state, of society as a whole. For all the public may be given the sense that the railways have become *their* railways, that transport is now provided as a form of public service, rather than as a means of private profit: may even feel they all share, in an infinitesimal and indirect way, in the success of the undertaking – at least no longer have to pay a gratuitous and unjustified surcharge into the maw of the private capitalist. Yet here too this does not necessarily imply that public ownership must take the form of state ownership. That sense will be given equally if the railways are run at the European level, or the Western Region level, so long as they are publicly run. Even if it is assumed that there must be a subsidy for such an industry (say for the railways today), this does not necessarily entail a state-wide industry, for there could be continental or regional or local subsidies. And this would still remain the case even if the state remained a main provider of funds: subsidies could either be subscribed from a national government to a continental railway system, or distributed from national governments to separate regional railway systems. Nor would the need, if there is one, to establish a national transport policy (or fuel policy) automatically dictate state-run industries: such policies could be designed to *co-ordinate* the activity of several regional undertakings as well as to run a single national corporation.

But if these arguments hold good of basic utilities of this kind, where there exists a strong case for monopoly, they are even more relevant to such industries as steel, shipbuilding, aircraft and other parts of manufacturing industry which are in many countries placed under public ownership. Here, where there is no self-evident reason for a monopoly at all, social ownership could as well take the form of several competing publicly-owned enterprises as a single, mammoth state corporation. Yet here too it is generally assumed that socialisation must mean nationalisation.

There is another, and quite separate, paradox surrounding the identification of socialism with increasing state power. One of the aims of socialists has been to create a more equal society – many indeed today hold that public ownership is mainly a means towards that end. Yet the establishment of industries in the hands of the state can scarcely be shown in itself to have brought about greater equality. In Britain the difference in income between the chairman of British Rail (or British Electricity or British Leyland) on the one hand and the lowest-paid worker in those undertakings on the other is not appreciably less now than it was when they were privately owned. In the Soviet Union, it has been commonly remarked, the differences in income and standard of living between the highest and lowest-paid is not significantly lower than between those holding similar positions in the West. In so far as there are less differences in income and wealth throughout society today in either country, it is not because of the extension of state ownership, but for entirely other reasons: because of the taxation and social service policies pursued. Social ownership in itself has contributed little to the process. Nor has it brought usually any greater equality in influence over management decisions.

Moreover, there is today another, and an increasingly important, reason why the extension of state ownership can have little effect in reducing inequalities. One of the principal features of the modern world, as will be discussed in greater detail later, is that increasingly inequalities have become *collective* rather than individual: between large collectivities, whose members share a similar destiny and a similar standard of living. Increasingly accumulation is not among individuals, as in the time when the early socialists wrote, nor even among corporations. Saving and investment today is above all undertaken by the state itself. Here too the state has taken control: through its power of taxation, from individuals and corporation alike, it absorbs into its hands increasing shares of the wealth of each community, and spends them collectively on behalf of the community as a whole.

The result is that the wealth and welfare of each citizen is today increasingly determined, not by his own actions, but by those of the state to which he belongs. It is the relative success of his own state in managing its economy, in stimulating its exports, in restraining its population, in promoting its growth, which will determine the relative prosperity of every citizen. Because the success of states varies greatly in this - as well as their starting-dates - so does the wealth of their citizens. So while, only a century or so ago, in India and the US alike there were some very wealthy people and some very poor, today, with only insignificant exceptions, *everybody* in the US is wealthier than everybody in India. Increasingly, all over the world, the prosperity of every citizen is determined not by his own endeavours and income but by those of his state. Inequality is not so much among individuals in the same state: it is between states themselves.

In such circumstances, the goal of concentrating the means of production, the sources of income and wealth, in the hands of the individual state becomes quite irrelevant to the task of securing greater equality among mankind. For even if public ownership in that form, that is the nationalisation of the means of production, distribution and exchange, were achieved in every country of the world, and even if it resulted in a far greater equality among the inhabitants of each of those nations (and, as we have seen, this has not normally been the result), it would have no effect whatever on the main inequalities that exist in the modern world: those that occur *between* states. Yet the difference in standard of living between India and the US, between Malawi and Sweden, between Nepal and West Germany, are infinitely greater than any that exist *within* any of these states. Moreover, those differences - unlike those that exist within states, which are generally lessening - are, in terms of income a head, becoming greater all the time.

These are therefore the inequalities about which socialists today should be most concerned. A form of social ownership that affects only inequality within states is quite irrelevant to reducing the most important inequalities of the modern world. Any political doctrine which is seriously concerned about the remedying of inequality may need therefore, for this reason too, considerable rethinking: may require quite a different interpretation of the meaning of the concept of social ownership – and so of socialism itself.

The political creed which has been primarily concerned about reducing inequality is thus, in its most commonly adopted form (the doctrine of state socialism), irrelevant to the main social problems which exist today. On the one hand, it has been unable to achieve many of the goals which have been hoped from social ownership within states – failed, that is, to increase equality, failed to abolish alienation, failed to provide any genuine sense of control for the worker over his own destiny, or for the citizen over the decisions which affect him. On the other, it has failed as a means for abolishing the inequalities of the modern world which are by far the most important in scale and effect.

If socialism is to be restored, therefore, as the most significant political doctrine of our age, as the faith which might resolve the worst predicaments of mankind in industrial society, and reduce the worst injustices of our world, some of its tenets may require to be radically reappraised.

Part I: The Triumph of the State

1 The Omnipotence of Organisation

1.1 *Power and Organisation*

Most history is about the growth of organisation: the progressive attempts of human beings to manipulate and organise each other in ever more complex ways. The primeval family, with only a handful of people seeking to meet all their own needs, gives way to the hunting horde with a dozen or twenty members, still only loosely organised. The pastoral tribe and the agricultural village, each with a hundred or two people, living as self-sufficient communities, give way to the more complex structure of the city-state, with a population of several thousands and an increasingly complicated division of labour. This in turn is replaced by the first empires, controlling much larger territories and extensive populations, regulated by the first legal codes and administered by a large bureaucracy of officials. Finally these in turn yield to the modern state, which gradually takes under its control more and more areas of human activity, establishes a vast apparatus of administration, and lays down a huge network of detailed regulations and controls on every citizen, while at the same time economic organisations, whether or not controlled by the state, also become ever greater in scale and ever more remote from those who work within them.

Though described in crude terms, this continuous trend is a reality. The progression to larger-scale organisation is not absolute or uninterrupted, but it is steady and inexorable. And in the last century or so, with the conquest of distance and advance of technology, it has become more rapid than ever. A century or two ago, relatively few people worked in organisations of more than ten people; and very large numbers worked entirely alone. Today few work alone, and the great majority work in organisations of over one hundred people: in many cases in organisations of thousands and tens of thousands. In this process each individual human being becomes gradually enmeshed in an ever-widening network of rules, roles and relationships: those required by the social, economic and political organisation to which he belongs. Increasingly people's actions are determined by the purposes and needs of the organisation, rather than by the freely chosen decisions of the individual himself.

The most basic of the processes that has been at work is the development of communications. Improved communications make it possible, first, to bring greater *areas* under centralised administration, and so to establish more detailed control of events at the periphery. In its simplest form this occurs through the increased possibility of military control: so that states the size of Russia and India, Brazil and China, eventually can today be administered as single states – something which would have been quite impossible until very recently (as the experience of China constantly proved). In a certain sense good communications are a *cause* of size: they make possible the conquest and administration of larger areas. But, equally, size itself may cause better communications, as these become necessary for the effective administration of a certain territory. The extent of the Roman empire caused Roman roads to be built, just as Roman roads made possible the administration and defence of the empire.

But in addition communications affect the *degree* of control maintained. Two hundred years ago, even in territories which had been conquered, most administration had to be left for local decision on the spot. Today, with the communications facilities available, detailed administrative decisions even for remote localities can be undertaken from a capital city many miles away. In the last century especially, the development of telegraph, telephone, radio, telex, air travel, communications satellites and other advances, with improved methods of *storing* information, such as punched-card systems, electronic machines and complex computers, have hugely increased the capacity for central control – as well as the economic advantages which result from it – both for governments and economic organisations. So the new communications systems not only make possible the extension of power over wider and wider areas, but the *retention* of that power by ever more complex administrative systems.

In a sense this process can be seen as the interaction of two trends: the extension of power and the extension of organisation. On the one hand, *individuals* have tried, singly or collectively, to attain for themselves, or for their group, a position of greater status, influence or wealth: and sought power over ever wider areas to attain them. On the other, the *authority* so established seeks to regulate the affairs of the group it controls in ever more detailed ways to attain functional objectives for the group as a whole.

Each of these processes is attainable only in so far as the communications allow them. When the mule is the only means of transport both power and organisation cannot extend beyond the village. With the aeroplane and the railway they may control territories as large as China or the Soviet Union. In some cases competition by individuals for power may lead to *reductions* in organisation: by increasing conflict and stress and therefore malfunction. Conversely the attempt to extend organisation may lead to reductions of individual power: by establishing collective leadership and subordinating individuals within more firmly defined roles. But normally the two processes reinforce each other. Attempts to extend power usually bring about a parallel extension in administrative organisation; while extensions of organisation, for example in larger-scale structures, often lead to extensions of power for a few individuals at the apex of authority as well.

The two forces join in seeking to impose order on society. The basic purposes underlying the two processes are distinct. One is regulated by individualistic and self-interested ends (whether of individuals or groups), for some at the expense of others; the other by social and co-operative objectives, conceived to be in the best interest of *all* (even if involving sacrifices for some). The one is largely haphazard or unpredictable in effect, depending on the interplay of individual self-assertion and competitive instincts; the other is deliberate, progressive, and, to some extent predictable. But both contribute to the same end-result: an increasingly complex and rigid organisational structure.

In recent times, the extension of organisation has increasingly displaced the extension of power. The discomforts and insecurities of an order resting primarily on the basis of individual whim, the gradual assertion by majorities within each society of their own rights and interests, the increasing acknowledgement of majority rights by the moral codes generally prevalent, greater understanding of administrative techniques and economies of scale, all these together have brought about systems of organisation in which large-scale purposes increasingly subordinate individual ends; in which competitive activities are more and more moulded and modified by communal goals. While there is still power at the top, and highly concentrated, it is power now conditioned and controlled by social objectives and socially imposed restraints. Legal, political, social and economic orders are established at wider and wider levels.

Such a trend has sometimes been classed as a movement towards increasing 'rationality',[1] but it is so only if rationality is identified as a *social* quality, presupposing large-scale organisation for common ends. Rationality is properly the choice of suitable means to achieve given goals; and the movement here described is rational for each individual only if the ultimate and long-term goals that *individuals* most highly value correspond with the ends sought by groups. But while the search for large-scale order has achieved certain goals widely and genuinely cherished, it is open to question whether the ultimate effect, in terms of the type of society and the way of life promoted, corresponds with the most deeply-held or long-term aspirations of individuals today.

Nor can this movement be defined as a simple development away from *communities*, intimate, structured and essentially organic, towards *societies*, open, contractual and basically mechanical.[2] In some cases (for example in some totalitarian states of recent times) an opposite trend has shown itself. A high degree of organisation is perfectly compatible with, and may even favour, a powerful sense of community and corporate loyalty. The essential effect of more complex systems of organisation is not in the type of loyalties created, the leadership principle adopted, or the sense of community maintained. The essential feature is the increasing proportion of personal relationships and activity which become conditioned and predetermined by collective goals, goals which the individual has little effective freedom to determine; and the increasingly powerful and pervasive socialisation required to undertake that conditioning. The total result is that, instilled through modern methods of education and modern communications media, the constraints imposed by collective demands – in working life, in administrative practices, in political organisation, even in social contacts – today exert a tyranny, though less cruel, more compelling than the tyranny previously wielded by personal rulers. For those could command men's bodies: not, as today's, their minds.

1.2 *Collectivisation of Interests*

Hand in hand with the growth of large-scale organisation has gone the collectivisation of interests.

Through much of history, authority within political systems was largely personal. It rested with individual rulers, kings, first ministers, prominent politicians or dictators, individuals who exercised a preponderant (though never a total) power or influence. But in most countries political history has seen a progressive challenge to such personal power by various sections of the population: the challenge to the king's power by the church and the nobles, the challenge to the power of these by the bourgeoisie, finally, the challenge to that of the bourgeoisie by the working population as a whole. Even during this period the personal leader – the Cromwell, the Napoleon, the Hitler, or the Stalin – could be a dominant influence and could change the course of history. But increasingly the quest has been not for personal power to promote personal interests, but for collective power, to promote the collective interests of the group.

The most obvious collective interest, traditionally, has been that of the 'class'. The nobles compel King John to sign the Magna Carta on behalf of the noble class generally; the parliamentary forces conquer and execute Charles I on behalf of the middle class; the trades union movement is organised, and the Labour Party established, to win power for the working class as a whole. Some social and political historians interpret most of history in terms of a 'class struggle' of this kind. Socialists in particular have traditionally regarded 'class conflict' as the primary force behind political change.

But in the contemporary world this traditional concept of 'class' becomes increasingly tenuous. What is a 'class' today? Should it be defined by income group, or occupation, or education? And where does one begin and another end? Is the worker who owns a few unit trust units a capitalist? Or the managing director who owns no shares a worker? For a class to have any clear identity, its members must feel themselves linked together in a way they are not linked to others.

Today there are few such clear-cut divisions. A man may recognise himself as a bus-driver as against a railwayman; as an assembly worker as against a craftsman; a clerk as against a manager; but not as a member of the 'proletariat' as against the 'property-owners', as he reasonably could in Marx's day. For the

railwayman may own a house, while the managing director may
be only a tenant. Nor is income a reliable guide. All those below a
certain level of income are not immediately visible as a group; they
are not clearly linked together to promote their interests; above all
they do not jointly negotiate against rival classes. A class today has
no organisation. It never meets. 'Class' is not even any longer easily
recognised, from the evidence of dress, speech, housing, or other
such signs. Above all, interests are not mainly *felt* in these terms
today: so consciousness of 'class' in the old-fashioned sense has
almost ceased to exist in most Western societies (though Britain,
because of its divided educational system, remains something of an
exception).

More important, however, than the decline of class-consciousness is the fact that other collective interests have emerged, which
are more significant in determining the welfare, income and life-
style of their members. One obvious group interest is that shared by
every individual with other fellow-workers in the same occupation-
group. Representatives of such groups *do* negotiate, at national
level or locally, on the wage-scales which determine their standard
of living and relative status. They meet together regularly (as
members of the same 'class' have never done, and could never do)
both at their places of work, in union meetings, and in national
conferences, to plan their strategy, to state their demands, and to
mobilise a sense of common purpose among their members. Their
common interest in seeking certain rates of pay and certain
conditions of work is manifest and concrete, and visible to
themselves, in a way that the vague and amorphous common
interest and purpose of the 'propertyless' or 'capitalist' class can
never be. But their interest as members of such an occupational
group cuts across that of members of other groups of the same kind.
Because the capacity of the economy as a whole is limited, a pay-
claim granted to railwaymen is to some extent, through higher rail
fares, at the expense of busmen and miners, whose standard of
living is thereby reduced. The skilled negotiate to maintain their
differentials against the less skilled, the less skilled to destroy them.
Because employers normally add the cost of the claim to the cost of
the product, rather than accepting a cut in profits or dividends, a
gain is secured by employees of one industry against those in all
others, rather than against their own employers.

Next, every individual has a collective interest in the success of
his own *enterprise*, whether public or private. To some extent at least

the success of the enterprise is a success for himself. Even if wage-rates are negotiated nationally, the amount of overtime he earns, the avoidance of short-time and dismissals, bonuses, welfare facilities, pensions, and other advantages depend on the success achieved by the firm. He may be given special bonuses on the basis of profits, or even own shares in the firm. Moreover today wage-rates, and still more salary-rates, often vary from firm to firm according to their success. A sense of common purpose among all in the same enterprise is fostered by the management through works magazines, works outings, public relations, sports activities and other means. Here again employers and employed often share a common interest, for example against rival firms. Successful representation by employers with the government, to win financial aid or to secure a contract at home or abroad, may benefit the workers as much as the employers, and so win their support. Government policies which adversely affect the firm will be resisted by both employers and employed. It is the common interest in the enterprise, whether public or private, that counts.

Thirdly, there is the collective interest of the *locality*. Even within states, economic interests are divided by region, as much as by birth or occupation. The important class distinctions in Britain today are between the privileged south and midlands, and the depressed north and outer regions. A similar regional division exists in almost every nation; between east and west in France, between west and east in Germany, between north and south in Italy, between prosperous coasts and less prosperous interior and south in the US. It exists in most countries between town and countryside. These divergencies between the wealth and amenities and services of different regions increase more quickly than those between occupational groups. Thus the collective interests which individuals share as a member of a particular locality or region – as Scotsmen or Bretons or Bavarians – become as important to them as their 'class' interest. Those of the same locality share an interest in new investment, new transport facilities, new regional policies, as important as their interest in a higher wage settlement. And in many countries this is reflected in the fact that a great part of political activity consists in procuring greater prosperity, new investment, new contracts, new grants, for the politicians' own region.

But the most important collective interest which individuals share today is that of the state to which they belong. This is important partly because the state is the chief agent of economic activity, on which the prosperity of all depends. The accumulation of funds, important investment decisions, the provision of services and amenities, general control of the economy and many other activities, once undertaken primarily by individuals for themselves, are now undertaken by the state on behalf of all. It matters far more to the economic interests of each citizen whether he has a government that can maintain full employment, or can achieve a 5 per cent rate of growth instead of a 2 per cent rate (and so greater take-home pay), than whether he himself works marginally harder, or whether his own union negotiates a more successful wage-claim. A larger and larger element of the standard of living of each individual is *social* – in highways, hospitals, housing, schools, protection and other services: provided by social decisions and social activity, rather than individually procured. Citizens today thus vote for one party rather than another mainly as the more or less efficient managers of the national economy as a whole, since this is what will determine their interests, rather than as the representatives of one class against another. Finally, because the largest differences in standards of living exist between those who live in different states, rather than between classes in the same state, the collective interest that individuals have as members of their own nation has become far more visible and far more important than the interest they have as members of any particular income group or profession; and this collective interest is reflected in the economic negotiations of states, both bilateral on tariffs and trade, and multilateral between rich countries and poor.

All of these group interests and rivalries have become more important, economically, politically and even socially, than those of the traditional 'classes'. One effect of large-scale organisation is that the individual becomes absorbed in the purposes of the organisation, the enterprise, the locality, the nation. His interests become collective. And his welfare today, in socialist and non-socialist states alike, is no longer determined by his own efforts or success so much as by those of the collectivity to which he belongs: above all, those of the state.

1.3 *The Collectivisation of Power*

Equally important with this collectivisation of interests is the collectivisation of power.

Because none will any longer trust the absolute power of individuals, the political process is collectivised. The personal and the arbitrary, which once were dominant political forces, are deliberately ironed out. Written constitutions, firm traditions, formal processes of election, prescribed legislative forms, judicial review, consultation with specified groups and bodies, these determine what changes can be made at any one time. Violence, revolution and all sudden change are banished from history.

Nations are increasingly ruled by collective bodies: cabinets, committees and chambers, rather than personal rulers, military dictators or reforming saviours. In Communist countries, as in the West, 'collective leadership' becomes the guiding principle. In developing countries, even when revolutions do take place, rule is often by a committee of officers, rather than, as once, by a single military dictator. Parliaments themselves become increasingly organised, disciplined and regimented. Anyway they count for little against the real power behind the scenes: the bureaucratic machine. There is little room for the independent member, even the independent-minded member, within most modern parliamentary assemblies; for all are the slaves of their party, another collective machine. This process of collectivisation induces a further hardening of the arteries of the political process. In a world of collectivised power, the *committee* becomes the characteristic ruler, the bureaucracy the characteristic instrument.

In the economic sphere, equally, power becomes collective. The personal entrepreneur, the innovator or the successful businessman, who made his personal fortune through his own efforts, energy and expertise, is today replaced by the corporation and company, controlled by the 'board', the directors and the professional managers; and here, too, behind the scenes, there are large bureaucracies of skilled advisers, accountants, engineers and planning staff. Enterprise becomes corporate rather than personal. At the wider level, economic life as a whole is increasingly controlled, even in non-socialist states, by the government and its army of advisers, acting through monetary policy, budgetary decisions, planning control and active intervention. More and more, the economic life of each community and of each enterprise is controlled, directed and planned by collective authorities, deciding from above, rather than being the end-product of large numbers of individual transactions, desires or decisions from below.

In both the political and economic sphere these trends can be seen as advances of a kind. Collectivisation represents a safeguard for the interests of the majority against arbitrary personal power. But that advantage has to be paid for at huge cost. Because power is made collective, it becomes more *legitimate*. A democratic state is, as a result, in some ways today more authoritarian than the most tyrannical autocracy in previous centuries. Invasions of liberty which might have seemed intolerable when practised by a personal ruler become acceptable when demanded by the 'majority'. So long as the correct constitutional forms have been followed, virtually anything becomes today permissible. State power is thus continually increased: for it is demanded by the established and legitimate authorities in the interest of 'all'. And the individual human being, in whose interests collectivisation took place, is continually further submerged or subordinated.

Thus while political theorists in earlier times were concerned to devise theories of 'natural rights' and the 'division of powers', to draw up carefully formed written constitutions to protect the individual and to limit the powers available to governments, in the twentieth century such limitations no longer seem necessary, or even desirable. On details, liberal premises may be accepted: literary censorship is relaxed, freedom of political expression and the formation of political parties is acknowledged, ombudsmen guard against the abuse of powers. But on the fundamentals, society becomes more totalitarian than ever. The volume of legislation perpetually increases, each law encroaching marginally on individual freedom. Though many are not *felt* as encroachments by individuals, this is only because all citizens are increasingly indoctrinated by the collective will, moulded by the pressures of society as a whole. The sanctification of majority rule involves the increasing submergence and assimilation of all minority views.

Collective power, institutionalised and legitimised in this way, has other effects. A democratic society, in the condition of modern mass communications, inevitably tends to be passive, even conservative. This is partly because the majority of humans are essentially passive and conservative, and a system reflecting majority views must therefore be so too. But it is mainly because electorates become more prepared to accept whatever government, the 'authorities', may decree. On the one hand, governments are remote, so that they cannot be easily influenced. On the other, because government decisions can be made to seem to represent a commonly accepted purpose, or are claimed to fulfil a mandate, the general willingness to submit is increased. When the king ruled, there were innumerable Wilkeses and Hampdens, Voltaires and Diderots, to preach defiance of royal authority. When the people rule, nobody feels justified in rebelling. The sense that decisions are self-administered leads to the assumption that they must be right. Power acquires a new legitimacy, based no longer on myth and symbol but on widely accepted democratic theory, the gospel of popular sovereignty. The populations of Communist states accept Communist rule as normal and right, just as passively as those in capitalist accept capitalist rule as normal and right. With a few (and diminishing) exceptions among the young, radical dissent is therefore less radical and less dissenting than in any earlier age.

Collective power is also conservative because, within the democratic system, political parties and leaders are obliged to converge to a point near the average views of the majority. Parties no longer seek to represent totally separate groups of divergent interests among the population. All aim to attract the votes of all. All compete in representing the *same* views; especially those of the middle, floating section which ultimately determines elections. More accurate knowledge of popular opinion and prejudices, now revealed more clearly than ever by public opinion polls, inhibits any views known to be in conflict with those of a majority of voters; while, conversely, those known to be shared by that majority are competitively canvassed more intensively than ever before. Because the majority are rarely in favour of important or imaginative changes, this inhibits any radical challenge to the *status quo*. Challenges to the system as a whole appear particularly subversive and taboo: so Communists diminish to an insignificant fringe-group in the West, just as pro-capitalists do in the East.[3]

Finally, the majority that becomes all-powerful is perpetually increased in size. Within national states, whole regions, ethnic groups and religious minorities are more and more submerged by unifying and centralising governments. On a world scale the growth of international government brings about a similar process: the need for co-ordination of national activities in many fields brings about, there too, the same demand for centralised regulation of national actions that once emerged within nations to regulate personal actions. Even on the world level, therefore, there emerges increasing centralisation of authority, increasing institutionalisation of power, increasing submergence of minority views and values in a single world consensus.

It is above all where *collective interests* have emerged (in the way we traced in the last section) that *collective power* will follow. So it is particularly in those forms we described – the economic organisation, the region and the state – that this collective power, the new source of authority, becomes crystallised. There is a mutual interaction. As groups find themselves to have a common interest in securing certain common ends, they create the organisation, political or economic, for achieving them; and as that organisation, through its own activity, increases in authority and power, its members increasingly identify with them as the agents of the ends they desire.

As a result of this process of collectivisation of power, therefore, there emerge fewer and larger organisations, each pursuing its own purposes, and each finally controlled in turn by a single all-dominant majority. Individuals and local groups, with their own divergent views and values, are increasingly swamped, submerged, suppressed, within the miasma of this all-powerful, middle-of-the-road consensus. Collectivities, rather than individuals, become henceforth the main political actors.

1.4 *Integration and the Individual*

For socialism the process we have described presents a special problem.

Socialists have always stressed that their fundamental concern is with the quality of human life. They have affirmed the superiority of human existence in a socialist society over that in a capitalist state. Man himself, it is said, is the final end. Political and economic organisation is merely the means to glorify and enrich that end. But the process of organisation – and human impoverishment – we have described affects capitalist and socialist states alike. If anything the collectivisation of life is still more pronounced in socialist societies. And yet that process of collectivisation itself nullifies the hope of a more satisfying human existence which socialism has always held out. The process of organisation threatens to become not a means to the end of creating a better way of life for all human beings, but an end in itself, for which human beings become merely the instruments. Increasingly the *downwards-*

moving movements in society, stemming from the organising process itself, are in danger of overpowering the *upwards-moving* movements, originating among individual men and women creating their own existences.

For, paradoxically, the three inexorable processes we have described – the search for order, the collectivisation of interests and the collectivisation of power – bring not an advance in human society but a reversion: to something like the efficiency of socialisation that existed in many primitive communities. Within those societies, too, there existed powerful pressures working towards conformity, the customary authority of the tribe or totem group. There too roles and rules were established which it was difficult for individuals to modify. For a time, the emergence of complex industrial societies, with many diverse sub-groups, the process of urbanisation and the accompanying detribalisation, the improvement in communication *between* societies, tended to reverse this process. New societies brought into existence a variety of separate reference groups, each having their own values and principles and ways of life, each exerting variable influences on the individual citizen. As a result social pressures were more haphazard and inconsistent in effect, and the individual's freedom of choice was enhanced. The emergence of individuals or groups proclaiming heterodox, non-conformist or deliberately rebel values became easier. And the constant incursions of foreign cultures, social systems and religious concepts brought the eruption of new influences, which stimulated perpetual challenges to the existing order.

Today each of these factors has become less significant. The breaking-down of the class system and the status-based society, and the increasing diffusion of a single popular culture and social order that results, have the effect that within the same society the co-existence of separate and interactive social and cultural systems is replaced by a single, uniform national culture: all watch the same television programmes, are subject to the same social influences. An increasingly consistent pattern of socialisation, and a homogeneous system of public education mean that fewer and fewer unusual individuals escape the common mould of indoctrination that modern societies impose. Finally, the breakdown of the division between separate national cultures and systems, and the increasing establishment of a common social, economic and administrative structure throughout the world, reduce the possibility of the emergence, through culture-contacts, of new values, ideals and ways of life to challenge the prevailing orthodoxy.

The domination of the all-powerful state above all reduces the possibility of dissent and diversity. If the process of increasing organisation continues and culminates, as now seems possible, in an integrated world state, or at least a world society, embracing all mankind, assimilation would go further. A social and political mechanism of such perfection and rigidity might emerge that it lost all capacity for change and enriching development. Deprived of those elements of diversity and individuality that have provided the most fertile stimuli in the past, imprisoned in the straitjacket of 'stability', human society could eventually become, like that of the ants and bees, a fossil, only marginally evolving over millions of years. Increasing order would become the foundation of security, but the negation of spontaneity; the basis of organisation, but the destroyer of originality; the instrument of material progress but the impediment to mental or spiritual development and diversity. Only a political and social system that deliberately sought to counter the organising, centralising trend, therefore, might serve to preserve diversity and spontaneity, and so to foster creative evolution.

Political thought has always been concerned about the ways in which men may manufacture political structures. It has been less concerned about the way political structures may manufacture men. Yet, precisely because the institutions men manufacture may come eventually to modify and control themselves, that study may be equally important to their political destiny. Because institutions enjoy a life more permanent and impregnable than the individual, because they can canalise his activities, mould his aspirations, create his expectations, and restrain his individuality, the study of these institutions and their influence may not only be essential to understanding his predicament, but may assist him to escape from the bondage they impose. So, just as understanding of man's physical nature may help him to escape from physical compulsion, and understanding of his psychological nature help him to find liberation from psychological necessity, understanding of man's political nature may help him to free himself from his political constraints.

This process of ever more complete human integration presents a special challenge to socialism. Nearly all the political dilemmas of the modern age – the remoteness of politicians and political authority, the power of the bureaucracy, the technical nature of many decisions and the consequent increase in the power of the expert, the individual's sense of alienation, the decline of truly local government, the difficulty of decentralising and sharing decision-making – all these are the direct result of this process of ever-widening and ever-encroaching organisation we have described: above all the increased power of the state. But socialism, in seeking the establishment of order and justice within states, has been concerned so far with the *extension* of state power and so of complex organisation. Today, if it is to be concerned about man himself rather than the state he inhabits, about human satisfaction rather than human organisation, socialism must begin to concern itself not only with securing order and justice (though these ends remain as essential as ever), but with how to secure those values with the least possible damage to the spontaneity and diversity which are the essential conditions of a satisfying human existence, but are increasingly threatened by the growing pressures towards still more perfect organisation.

2 The Take-over of Socialism by the State

2.1 *Socialism Becomes State Socialism*

The main beneficiary of the process of increasing organisation we have described has so far been the state.

National governments, each ruling individual national territories, have extended their power into ever more detailed areas of everyday life. In theory this process of creating ever wider systems of administration and economic management could lead eventually to the establishment of a single, highly integrated world state. This might come about both as a means of achieving the yet more efficient accomplishment of functional tasks; and to secure a more just distribution of wealth and welfare throughout the world.

But if the attempt to establish such a world state was undertaken by one state seeking to extend its own power, others would certainly resist it. This could occur therefore only at a cost in human life that no state at present seems likely to contemplate. If a world state is to come about, therefore, it will be by the *voluntary* relinquishment of power by national governments to international bodies. And that process, if it occurs, will be long and slow.

Thus today the national state continues to wield supreme power, subject to little challenge. In a few cases, mainly in less developed regions, states are challenged by minority groups, political or ethnic, within their territories. But even then in almost every case it is the central governments which come out victorious, and successfully defend their authority (Cuba and Indo-China are possibly the only exceptions, where central governments defending their authority have been defeated, in recent times). And even where a government is, in such cases, defeated, it is merely replaced by another which asserts an equally omnipotent state power. Since governments today possess an overwhelming superiority of military power in their own hands, and since the acquisition of the modern weapons capable of challenging that power is beyond the means of most rebel organisations (unless powerfully supported from outside, as in Vietnam), the likelihood is that existing governments (and so existing *systems* of government) will normally be able to maintain themselves in control with little difficulty.

It is indeed not so much the existence of the state (which we can scarcely expect to see pass out of existence in the immediate future) that is the problem. It is the total *monopolisation* by the state, over the past century or so, of every shred of authority in every field of activity. The state has become in modern times the all-powerful, all-purpose, omni-competent organisation which totally rules men's lives. And yet it is, in the eyes of most men, a vast, impersonal, inhuman and almost abstract machine, that is not only – except in a most theoretical sense – beyond their control, but corresponds in no way with what they feel to be their own, immediate, living community.

By equating socialism with *state* ownership, therefore, modern socialist thinking serves only to intensify this discrepancy between authority and community. The organisation of industrial and other enterprises by the state, in addition to all the other areas of administration it controls, has the effect that social ownership ceases to be, as was once dreamed, a means of providing for the worker a social satisfaction, a sense of sharing in a common activity, a feeling that he can participate in decisions affecting his life. On the contrary, the state's monopoly of power, which under state socialism is even more total than elsewhere, has left him as alienated from society, from the community in which he dwells, as it has from the labour he contributes in the service of the state.

There are four benefits that writers and thinkers in early times mainly hoped would result from the establishment of a socialist system.

They hoped, first, that in such a society the individual citizen's activity would no longer be mainly self-seeking and self-regarding, designed to procure private profit and personal advantage, but would be socially directed: cooperation would replace competition as the basic motive of human society. Working life would be transformed into a joint effort for the benefit of all. Its main dynamic would be the sense that it was undertaken in the spirit of comradeship and mutual help for the sake of society as a whole. Yet it is doubtful if today, in the socialist states which have been established, or in individual socialist enterprises elsewhere, such a spirit is any more visible than in the capitalist undertakings of the previous era. The worker in the nationalised mines or railways in

Britain, or the worker in state-owned industry in East Europe, works just as much for his weekly wage packet as his fellow-worker in capitalist industry. He has little sense that he is engaged in a cooperative effort with and on behalf of all his fellow-citizens. His consciousness has not been transformed as early socialists, such as Robert Owen and Marx, once hoped. The reason is simple. It is not because of 'betrayal' by his leaders of socialist ideals nor even the failure to provide 'workers' control' in such states. It is above all the *scale* of operations, the remoteness of management, the number and anonymity of his fellow-workers, which has this effect. And this remains unchanged despite the change in ownership and control. Indeed, the worker in the small capitalist family firm, where human relations are sometimes close and warm, is often more likely to enjoy the satisfaction of harmonious cooperative endeavour than the worker who feels himself to be nothing but a tiny cog in a vast state-run corporation.

Secondly, in socialist industry, it had been hoped, the worker would be less *dependent* on the decisions of others than in private industry. He would no longer be merely a tool, the instrument used by the employer for his private profit, but become a self-directed, free individual, able himself to control his own destiny and the decisions which affected it. Yet, again, it is doubtful whether the worker in a nationalised industry today in Britain, or in the socialist systems of East Europe, feels any less dependent on the decisions of remote managers, feels any more a sense of self-direction or control of his destiny, than do those in private industry in the West. Even where attempts have been made to devise systems in which workers enjoy a share in management in socialist societies (as in Yugoslavia), these have not been uniformly successful and in some cases have been partially abandoned and the authority of management restored. Nor is there any significant difference between the operation of such schemes in socialist societies or socialist industries, and those for 'participation' in private capitalist firms in the West, as are increasingly practised (see pp. 117–22). In neither case have they significantly changed the worker's situation, or provided any real sense that he can influence or control the decisions of management, any more than his predecessors in more primitive capitalist systems.

Thirdly, it had been hoped, a special characteristic of socialist labour, transforming the life of the worker in socialist society, would be that the reward from his efforts would be justly shared.

Since there would be no private profit, no 'surplus value' stolen away from the worker, he would enjoy full participation in the success of the enterprise and share fully in the rewards it earned. He would thus obtain a more meaningful satisfaction (whatever his rate of pay) than the worker in capitalist society who received only the crumbs from the rich man's table, watching the private shareholder taking the profits he won through his labours. Yet again it is hard to think that the average worker in British Leyland or British Steel today enjoys any genuine feeling that he is fully participating in the success of the enterprise for which he works, still less that he can personally share in its profits, or those of the state, in a way that the worker in capitalist enterprise cannot. Though there may be no dividend to be paid out to the shareholders, there may be payments on fixed interest stock, which appear to the worker little different. And even if there are no such payments, he may still feel that the disbursement of huge salaries to the top managers in his nationalised industry, or of enormous sums to provide lavish carpeting and equipment in headquarters offices, or to finance expensive advertising campaigns, or even payments to the state itself, subtract from the rewards that he can earn as much as the profits of the firm or the shareholder's dividends withdraw rewards from the worker in capitalist industry. Certainly he does not normally find that he earns more than the worker in private industry. Nor is the distribution of income significantly different within the state enterprise.

Finally, socialists have hoped that in a socialist state the whole character of society will be changed and the assumptions of a selfish commercialism abolished. Yet even this hope is not fulfilled. The ethos of commercialism survives the change in industrial ownership. In a semi-socialist society such as Britain today, even though half of industry may be in public hands, the values of a commercial, even a fully capitalist, society continue to dominate everywhere. Strident commercialism, in the forms of ubiquitous advertisements and slogans insistently battering the captive consumer with their crude and self-interested exhortations, dominating the street, the newspaper and the sitting-room, is not only as universally evident as in the fully-fledged capitalist countries of North America, but has become far more pronounced than in the superficially more capitalist society of fifty years before (and many who call themselves socialists in Britain and other West European countries still cheerfully call for yet more advertisements in the sitting-room rather than finance television as a public service). Even the fully communist society uses the techniques of advertising to dragoon the consumer into the habits the state ordains and to inculate the tastes that it approves. The character of life is unchanged therefore. The spirit of a commercial society persists everywhere.

Whatever benefits it may bring for society, therefore, whatever advances in economic efficiency, state socialism provides for the *worker* in state industry few of the advantages which were traditionally claimed for it. The quality of life for those who live their lives in the service of socialist *enterprises* is at present barely distinguishable from that of those who live their lives in the service of capitalist employers. The style of living in a socialist *society* is barely distinguishable from that in a capitalist society. If the ideals of early socialist thinkers are to be realised, therefore, it can only be under some system of organisation different from that which has been practised so far under the system of state socialism.

2.2 *Bureaucracy Takes Control*

The conquest of socialism by the state has another effect. An entire national economy requires detailed control. Power at the top becomes highly concentrated: in a new oligarchy, a new high-priesthood, the privileged source of authority and wisdom. While *private* authority, acquired by inheritance or by wealth, is largely done away with, it is now replaced by the authority of a new meritocracy, acquired by examination success. Power is no longer wielded by the charismatic leader, who could win and retain authority by the force of his own personality, wisdom or political skills. Nor is it held by traditional potentates, holding it by virtue of heredity or ceremonial office. Nor can it even to any extent be retained by elected representatives of the people in parliament, and those to whom they entrust cabinet office; for these are expert only in the art of politics: in the complex tasks of administration, which become so much more important, they are totally dependent on the advice of their officials. The authority of the king, the dictator, the chief minister, even of cabinet and parliament, is now increasingly wrested from them by the new mandarins, the top administrators, whose task may be formally only to advise, but whose advice in practice becomes increasingly tantamount to the decision itself.

This is to some extent true in all states. It results from the advance of large-scale organisation we examined in the last chapter. The increasing complexity and technicality of modern government makes such a shift of power almost inevitable. The decisions to be reached within complex contemporary societies require a very high level of expert knowledge. They cease to be mainly any longer questions of principle, which can be determined by individual leaders, with or without reference to popular wishes, on the basis of immediate instinct or party programmes. They require detailed and careful analysis of a large volume of complicated factors bearing on the decision.

Only the bureaucrats possess the necessary expertise to make judgements on such matters: partly because they are chosen (like Chinese mandarins) as an intellectual elite in the first place, but mainly because they spend the greater part of their lives in day-to-day contact with a relatively narrow area of policy. Political leaders therefore rely increasingly on such judgements and advice. Their own authority depends partly on the fact that they are known to have access to this. And not only the leaders but parliament, press and public too are increasingly deferential towards such experts, increasingly unable to resist their authority, or even present alternative proposals, because they cannot compete with the assumed knowledge and experience of these advisers. So the political leaders become increasingly merely the mouthpiece for the mandarins who themselves make or mould the decisions (it is indeed only in mouthing, that is, explaining and justifying, decisions that the politician's expertise lies). So more and more the bureaucrats make the decisions, and rely on the politicians only to explain them to the public.

Of course the ministers loudly insist that authority remains firmly in their hands; that they merely seek advice, ask for alternative options to be presented to them, and then decide for themselves what should be done. But even if they genuinely believe this to be the case (and many do not), it is increasingly a delusion, comparable to that of the man on the station platform who blows a whistle whenever he sees a train leave, and then persuades himself that he has caused it to move. The skilled public servant, whether in central or local government, has acquired one art above all; that of presenting advice in a way that invites only one conclusion. The evidence that favours one course is heightened and enhanced, the evidence that might favour another is weakened or suppressed.

Since the minister himself cannot possibly know, in highly technical areas, all the detailed evidence which is relevant, the case which the bureaucrats favour must be adopted: for in the light of the facts, as they present them, it is the only rational course. In a highly technical world, therefore, ultimate power rests with those who are acknowledged as the experts.

This concentration of power results not only from the technicality, but also from the scale of modern government and modern enterprises. The top administrators of a government department take decisions that affect the lives and actions of hundreds of thousands who work under them, and of many millions who are affected by its activities. The managing directors of a large corporation – whether private (IBM or ICI) or public (the Coal Board or the Steel Corporation) – now chosen as experts rather than as enterprisers or leaders of men, as accountants or engineers rather than as successful tycoons or union leaders, take decisions that immediately determine the destinies of countless employees throughout the country. A very few members of regulatory bodies, such as the Civil Aviation Authority or the BBC, take vitally important decisions which affect the entire population. Yet none of the members of any of these bodies are elected. They are in practice responsible to no one. They rarely even have to explain their actions. Thus a small group of administrators, scattered in a few committee rooms and board-rooms in the capital, take most of the key decisions which determine the lives of the whole population.

But it is in the system of state socialism that this domination by the bureaucrats and top experts is most pronounced. For, put into effect in its fullest form, as in the Soviet Union for example, that system means that all the activities of the country become subject to the decisions or 'advice' of the top hierarchy of administrators. It is not merely that the whole of every industry is in many cases run by a single state corporation. Even if there are a number of competing state enterprises, as in Yugoslavia say, their actions and decisions may still require to be vetted and approved by a Ministry of Heavy Industry, or a Ministry of Electrical Power in the capital. Bureaucratic authority is thus still further enhanced.

Other features of state socialism have the same effect. In such a society – even in one only advancing towards socialism, such as Britain today – there are established an increasingly elaborate network of state institutions to undertake services of many kinds.

Enormous welfare agencies are established, complex tax systems to redistribute the wealth obtained from individuals and corporations, and many other nation-wide institutions, investment boards that determine the distribution of investment. Each of these requires a vast administrative machine, which again is run by hugely powerful bureaucrats, only spasmodically overseen by ministers.

In government and in industry alike, therefore, the growth in the scale of organisation, above all under a system of state socialism, gives rise to a proliferation of bureaucracy. This grows continually, both in terms of the numbers employed and in terms of the power which they can wield. At the top of each bureaucratic pyramid, in the government department and the large corporation alike, there exists always a small managerial elite who reach decisions that determine the lives of millions of people. Neither in industry nor in administration is this elite in any real sense accountable. In a democratic state the decisions of top bureaucrats may may seem to be controlled by their minister who is in turn responsible to parliament. But the automatic assumption by ministers of responsibility for decisions which they knew nothing whatever about, taken together with the weakness of parliament in relation to the executive, means that this responsibility to parliament is purely fictitious. Similarly in private industry the managerial elite is theoretically responsible to shareholders for the decisions they reach. But in practice the shareholder, lacking the expertise of the managers, and rarely willing to assemble in numbers that could outvote the managerial clique, will passively accept, except in the most glaring cases, whatever justifications are presented to them for the conduct of the company's affairs. Still less can the 'supervisory boards', and other institutions recently established or proposed to represent the workers within an industry or firm, exert any significant influence on the decisions reached. Here too the expert – in this case the top manager – is held to know best, and so in practice rules the roost.

Thus in every modern society, with power increasingly concentrated in the state, the authority of the bureaucracy becomes supreme. But this is so above all in the socialist state – where, that is, socialism has become state socialism – since the authority of the state and state officialdom is there particularly powerful. Far from the individual being liberated and made free with the coming of socialism in such states, he is made subject, even more than elsewhere, to the arbitrary and invisible authority of the all-wise, all-powerful bureaucracy.

2.3 *Specialisation*

But the technical and complex character of modern society affects not only the power of top administrators. It transforms the lives of the citizens with whom they deal, for they too, if less expert, also become, like the bureaucrats, increasingly specialised in their activities and impoverished in their lives.

Marx and Engels were inclined to regard the division of labour as a product of the capitalist system of production. They looked forward to a new Utopian socialist society, in which men would fish in the morning, hunt in the afternoon, study in the evening and discuss at night. The constraints placed upon the worker by the capitalist, seeking to use him as a personal tool for his own profit, would be removed. The worker would be freed to choose his own activities according to his own inclinations.

Unhappily the experience of state socialism until today shows few examples of working days passed so entrancingly. The division of labour is not visibly different in socialist states today from what it is in capitalist states at a similar stage of development. In both cases that division is now far more complex and more minutely subdivided even than it was in the societies known to Marx and Engels. In both capitalist and socialist states, the increasing scale and increasing complexity of modern society has led to an ever-growing specialisation in work.

There are three major developments in this field over the past century. Modern technology has led to a very rapid increase in the *number* of specialised occupations. Operations formerly performed by a single person (say, shoemaking) may today be performed in large industrial undertakings employing hundreds of operators who each perform separate operations, each at different rates of pay. The current classification of occupations in Britain contains altogether about 30,000 occupations: that of 1851 contained only 470. The rate of pay and the status associated with each of the modern grades diverge only marginally from the next. There is a fairly continuous spectrum from the very bottom to the top. In a sense, a larger and larger proportion can be said to belong, in terms of income and way of life, to a single class. Yet they are subdivided into hundreds of thousands of separate groups and interests according to the type of work they perform.

Secondly, a larger proportion of the new specialised occupations fall in the *middle* ranges of income and status. White-collar workers, skilled technicians, draughtsmen, teachers and other middle groups are the main growing elements in the population. The proportion of industrial workers in the US, having remained fairly stable at a little over 30 per cent for the last century, is now slightly declining. The proportion of agricultural workers has declined in nearly all developed states from 30 to 40 per cent to under 10 per cent and sometimes much less. The really big increase has come in white-collar and service workers of all kinds, who have increased from about 7 per cent to well over 50 per cent and are still increasing. Among industrial workers themselves a larger proportion become skilled or supervisory.

Thirdly, social mobility between classes, though somewhat greater than before, remains restricted. In most previous centuries the vast majority of the population have grown up into roughly the same social class and income grouping as their parents. Though this is slightly less so now, even today mobility is limited in the extreme. It is restricted by heredity, by educational opportunity, by cultural background, as well as by a number of conventional factors. There seems to have been surprisingly little change over the past sixty or seventy years in total mobility.[1] Nor is there a great difference among industrial societies.[2] In socialist and in capitalist societies alike there is not merely an increasingly complex hierarchy at any one time: that hierarchy tends to be transmitted, little changed, from one generation to the next.

The most important result of this increasing specialisation in modern societies is the consequence for individuals. Complex organisations impose more and more detailed roles on each category of worker, leaving less and less room for personal initiative. Increased interdependence means there is less chance for individual choice or spontaneity. Organisational procedures now become the rulers, as tyrannical as personal rulers before them.

The number of marginally different roles that can be performed may be larger. But there is less *variety*, both within them and between them. Different roles can be combined by the same individual in different ways. But this still brings little variety since the roles themselves are so similar. The total range of experience open to each person is often wider, with increased means and opportunity of travel, but the range of possible experiences is smaller. There seems to be a kind of second law of socio-dynamics at work, analogous to the comparable law of thermodynamics: the progressive extension of organisation in ever more fields of activity, with ever more efficient procedures for instilling required responses, tends (without countervailing forces) to bring about decreasing scope for individuality and spontaneity; and so leads in time to the progressive stereotyping of personalities and experience.

But this process is in no way changed under socialism: there is no discernible difference in this respect between socialist and capitalist societies nor between socialist and capitalist enterprises. In both, the way of life of those who work there becomes continually more uniform. If anything the degree of subordination, the lack of opportunity for individual initiative, is greater in socialist states. The liberating effect which Marx and others hoped would result from the abolition of property has not been seen. Actions and attitudes are increasingly imposed on all by the demands of the organisation, rather than by the needs of the individual human being.

2.4 *Socialisation by the State*

Having gradually and inexorably extended its power into every field of activity, having spawned its top hierarchy of bureaucracy to maintain the machine so created, having imposed increasingly specialised roles on all its citizens to keep that machine in motion, the modern state also undertakes a process of intensive socialisation among its citizens to maintain its supremacy, far more thorough than any undertaken before.

Once again this results at root from the improvement in communications of every kind. It is clearly communication which mainly conditions the kind of socialisation that can be instilled: the type and amount of messages transmitted within a society, both from government to people and among the population. Until quite recently, most information has been transmitted by word of mouth. Information of this kind within a primitive tribe, information repeated with considerable uniformity and intensity, could establish a fairly rigid social order, but over a limited area only. Within an agricultural village, communication might depend on intermittent door-to-door gossip, or common attendance at religious services and other ceremonies, among a more scattered population, less frequent and intensive: this perhaps allowed a greater degree of individual variation, but still maintained the norms established over a limited area only. Even in eighteenth-century Europe, news of the affairs of state or international developments percolated largely by hearsay for the vast majority of the population. Newspapers, in so far as they existed at all, were read by a very small class, who in this way obtained both a volume and a type of knowledge not available to the mass of the population. And there were still few ways for governments to address their peoples directly.

In modern societies the number of messages has risen many times. New methods of transmitting information have enormously increased the amount of information (including political information) available, and the numbers it reaches. Mass communications reach a very large proportion of the population in a short space of time. Through these means populations learn far more about the government of their country than ever before. But the important change is that they are now subjected to a barrage of messages mainly emanating from a single capital city, often presenting only a single set of political attitudes or attitudes that only marginally change with a change of government. Even if only a relatively small proportion derive either directly or indirectly from the government, a government may through them influence their populations more deliberately than they could in any previous time. This is seen in its most extreme form in totalitarian states – Hitler's Germany or Russia today. But in almost all states it takes place to some extent. In many, governments broadcast on radio and TV; often there is government influence over the press; or influence is exerted by press advertising and other means. Press conferences, government statements and announcements – 'news management' – are used to influence the population in favour of the government's policies and views.

More important, though, than the diffusion of government views by these means is the diffusion of common *attitudes*. For another effect of mass means of communication in modern societies is that the communication is concentrated: the total number of *sources* of common information over a large area is smaller. As a result, in both socialist and non-socialist states there is probably greater consistency in the type of viewpoint, knowledge and ideas acquired by populations of each state than ever before. Virtually a whole population today watches the same television programmes and reads the same newspapers every day of the year. The same words are read or spoken in every sitting-room of the land. The culture and way of thinking of society as a whole thus continually become more uniform. Particular groups, especially those controlling these media, may influence large sections of the population more immediately and more consistently than was possible in earlier societies. A Lord Beaverbrook or a Randolph Hearst, even a well-known TV commentator, can influence the opinion of millions of citizens in a way that has rarely been possible for any single individual to do before. In earlier times individual rulers have been able to control men's actions; but not their ideas, their entire image of the world, as now.

The third effect of the mass means of information is that news and opinions are increasingly *nationalised*. While there is very considerable variation in views and information presented in different states (and especially in different continents), there is only a marginal variation in those presented in the same states. This is reinforced by corresponding changes in the educational system, another major source of information that too is largely controlled by governments. Those living within the same country thus today normally have only marginally differing pictures of the world – and often only marginally varying political opinions from each other. But those living in Britain will have a totally different world-view from those living in China, those living in Egypt from those living in Australia; and so on.

So, in many subtle ways, those who read the same newspapers, watch the same television programmes, begin to feel a sense of something in common, feel themselves different from those who read other newspapers, watch different programmes. Above all, they all are conscious that they share common membership of a single political unit, whose decisions shape their lives. More and more the purposes of the state become their purposes.

In this way, the authority of the state, and the loyalty to it of those who live within it, are further enhanced in socialist and non-socialist states alike. Not only is a powerful bureaucracy created at the top to make or influence all the important decisions; not only are the citizens organised into increasingly specialised roles to make them better adapted to implement those decisions; increasingly powerful socialising agencies encourage the citizen to adopt a national consciousness, to take for granted the reality of state power.

In these circumstances it is scarcely surprising, given the role of the state everywhere, that in socialist thinking socialism everywhere comes to mean state socialism; that social ownership is taken to mean national ownership; and that the extension of social ownership means an extension of state power. Everywhere the supreme aim of socialism comes to be the socialist *state*.

3 The Decline of Community

3.1 *Socialism and Community*

Among the most deeply held beliefs of the early socialist writers was the contention that a socialist organisation of society would create among those who worked in it a new sense of community. In one of his early manuscripts Marx wrote:

> When communist workmen associate with one another . . . they acquire a new need, the need for society – and what appears as a means becomes an end . . . The brotherhood of man is no mere phrase with them, but a fact of life, and the nobility of man shines upon us from work-hardened bodies.[1]

The social ownership of the means of production, therefore, though important in itself, was mainly a means to a more important end: an expression of the desire, held by many political writers from Plato and Aristotle onwards, for a form of political organisation in which the essentially social nature of the human being could be most fully expressed.

Here once more, socialism in its modern form, and the socialist states that have actually been established, seem a long way from realising the goal that socialist theory has laid down. It seems doubtful whether, in the Soviet Union today, or even in China and Yugoslavia, there exists any more genuine sense of community than in capitalist states.

There are two separate ways in which a sense of community might have been realised in socialist states. One is through a strong sense of common sentiment, common purpose and common labour among all those working within the same enterprise. The other is through a strong sense of common sentiment, common purpose and common labour among the inhabitants of the same socialist state. There is reason to doubt whether, in either of these forms, a sense of community has been deeply established in any modern socialist state.

3.2 *Technology and Working Relationships*

Let us consider, first, relationships within the place of work. Clearly the nature of work relationships will always be directly affected by technological factors. Marx believed that technology – the forces of production – determined a somewhat vague concept which he termed the 'relations of production'. By this term he and Engels did not mean merely relationships within the factory or enterprise. They meant rather the relationships between the enterpriser (whether or not he was himself a manager) and the worker; and above all between enterprisers as a class and workers as a class. Under capitalism the forces of production would demand an increasing volume of capital investment; and this would bring about an increasing concentration of capital, an increasing surplus of labour, an increasingly low return on capital, an increasing pauperisation of the worker, leading eventually to the collapse of the entire system.

The fact that this particular forecast – the central, and indeed almost the only specifically *Marxist* element in socialist thought – has not been fulfilled need not here concern us. The significant point is that Marx was concerned here with the effects of the forces of production, that is technology, on relations in society as *a whole*. He never seriously examined the effect of the level or type of technology on relations within the individual *enterprise*, within the place of work. But that is where changes in technology will most affect relationships. And if one of the objects of a socialist system is to transform human relations at work, as well as within society as a whole, it is necessary to consider exactly how relations within the place of work are affected by different levels of technology and by different forms of organisation.

There is certainly little evidence that, in the socialist societies so far established, or in the socialist enterprises set up in Western states, working relations are significantly different from those in capitalist enterprises. In both cases there are directors (in boards or in ministries), managers at various levels, foremen or supervisors, charge-hands and workers. There is a generally similar type of hierarchy, a similar chain of command, a similar method of transmitting decisions from the top to the bottom. Nor are working conditions significantly different in the two cases. There exist in both cases the same huge numbers of workers in each enterprise, each knowing only a handful of his fellow-workers, each lost in the

vast anonymous crowd of employees as a whole, the same vast
shop-floors, the same bleak canteens, the same periodic abrupt
confrontations between workers and management (even if these
are not so publicly expressed in the socialist states of East Europe).

The worker in socialist states may just as much feel that he is
merely the instrument of the system, that production has become
an end in itself, rather than being closely directed to human needs;
may feel just as acutely the loss of the craftsman's pride in his work,
and in the self-directed art which he can bring to it. If there is
'dehumanisation' in the one case, there is in the other too. For the
dehumanisation derives not from the system of ownership but from
the system of management; and the system of management derives
at least in part from the scale of the enterprise and the numbers of
those employed. Only the adoption of a totally different technology, requiring only small-scale workshops, with a small number of
workers all reasonably familiar with each other – or a wholly
different system of organisation *within* the same factories, with
small groups of workers controlling their own activities by joint
decisions within a larger organisation – would bring about a
significant change in the 'relations of production'; would, that is,
transform the relationships in the workplace in the way earlier
socialists hoped.

Of course it can be held that those states we know so far are
imperfect socialist states; and imperfect socialist industries and
enterprises. Yet there is no evidence that the establishment of a
system of state socialism, the taking into national ownership of all
industry, or a single industry or firm, could ever be expected, alone
and in itself, to transform human relations, either in society as a
whole, or in the individual place of work. For the fact is that the
'dehumanisation', the remoteness, the alienation, the *anomie*,
which the modern industrial worker, and indeed the modern
citizen generally may experience, is not the effect of the system of
ownership, but of the scale of organisation and the numbers of
people who are involved in the production process.

The greater the numbers employed, the more complex will be
the hierarchy, the more remote and impersonal the system of
command and communication. The more advanced the technology, the more elaborate the division of labour. And this will in
itself make difficult the creation of the wholly new, more human,
more equal relationships which many have demanded from a
socialist economy.

The aim of establishing such new relationships remains as relevant and as important as ever. But there is no evidence that they will automatically result from altering the ownership of the means of production alone.

3.3 *Modern Industrial Society*

Nor is it only at work that the feeling of community has declined. In the modern state few citizens feel a sense of community with their fellow-citizens, with society as a whole either. And this, again, is as true of socialist as of non-socialist states today.

Once again it is not the system, but the scale of organisation which has this effect; which destroys any genuine sense of common social purpose, or common endeavour. It is the size of the state, the number of its population, the unstructured character of political and social life, the remoteness of authority, the drabness of townscapes and urban living conditions, that destroy the feeling of an integrated, living, social organism. And these are the same in socialist as in non-socialist societies.

A sense of community is certainly not established by the simple act of doing away with private property, as Marx and others seemed sometimes to suggest. In socialist societies there may be more propaganda intended to *instil* a sense of social consciousness and social responsibility. But it is unlikely that this significantly counteracts the many factors in the modern industrial state which erode the feeling of community.

First, such a sense is prevented to a large extent by the mere size of the population in most modern states. In the tiniest states of all, a sense of community may exist to some extent; say in Andorra or Liechtenstein. But as soon as the population rises over 100,000 or so any sense of intimacy, of fellow-feeling among citizens, must rapidly decline. Most states are thus far too populous to represent communities in themselves. But since the population of socialist states is no less than that of capitalist states, they too cannot, by the mere fact of being socialist, overcome this difficulty.

Secondly, in modern times, even within his own town, even in his own street, the citizen does not know most of those he lives with. He may not even know, except on nodding terms, those who live in the house next door or in the flat below. In many cases, unless he lives in a small village, he probably takes part in few social activities which bring him into contact with those within his neighbourhood. He may well live the greater part of his leisure life within this own sitting-room, in front of his own television set. At work he may know the man who works in the same room, or on the next machine. But many of his other workmates will be almost total strangers. All this is not significantly different in a socialist society; the ideal of a sharing society, of a group voluntarily working together for the common good, which is at the heart of socialist belief, is no more realised there than in Western states.

Similarly, the citizen today does not (except possibly at a time of national crisis) have a sense of common *purpose* with his fellow-citizens generally, known or unknown. This is partly because neither they nor he have any significant share in *choosing* the purposes of the state. Even if it is formally 'democratic', and even if he voted for the party that is in power (and he may not have done), it is that party's leaders, not he himself, who chooses its policies: he merely assents to them. Neither in the deciding of the main aims of government, nor in the detailed *discussion* of policy questions which may arise from day to day, does he have any significant share at all.[2] How should he therefore have any sense of community, even with his leaders, still less with his fellow-citizens, most of whom he does not know, and with whom he certainly never has the chance to discuss the affairs of his society? And the situation is no different in contemporary socialist states. Indeed in such states he usually has even less chance than elsewhere of choosing common purposes and discussing common problems.

The sense of social cohesion, group loyalty and group activity which characterised most earlier societies, where all the members of a living community, dwelling in close proximity to each other, knew each other, and joined in common activities together, today is lost therefore. This sense is found in the modern world only in the small village. Yet all over the world it is precisely the population of villages that is declining, while their inhabitants drift to great cities where the genuine social values have disappeared. Once arrived in the city, the citizen becomes a passive spectator, waiting on the decisions and actions of others, rather than himself being able to initiate actions for his community, as he could within the village from which he came. And yet, again, there is no reason to suppose the inhabitants of socialist cities are any more fortunate in this respect.

If human relationships are not significantly different in socialist societies from what they are elsewhere, it is because the basic social system has been unaltered. The growing concentration of authority in the state and state institutions, the dominance of the bureaucracy and other elites, the complex system of organisation, the inability of the vast mass of the population to affect the decisions reached by their leaders, the increase in scale, the impersonal character of city life, remain exactly the same as before. The anonymity which has often been remarked in modern industrial societies, the sense that the individual is lost in a vast crowd, few of whose members he knows personally, the otherness of authority, all these are no different from before. The concentration of power is usually even greater. The sense of community is as absent as in any other type of modern society.

It cannot therefore be said that a change in the ownership of the means of production in itself has served to bring about any fundamental transformation of relations within society as a whole, any more than it has brought about a change in relationships within the workplace.

3.4 *The Remoteness of Authority*

If the sense of community – the sense of a sharing in common purposes, activities and values – has been crushed in contemporary society, therefore, it is because of the size and power of the modern state, rather than of any particular system of ownership or industrial organisation. That growth in scale, the increasing remoteness of governing bodies from the governed, has taken place in all types of society, irrespective of political philosophy and economic organisation. Only in a small number of developing countries – in China and Tanzania for example – have there been conscious efforts to promote organisation at the local level which can more closely reflect popular consciousness and loyalties. And even there the local units have often been increasingly overlaid by inexorable centralisation, made necessary, it is held, by the need for administrative efficiency and economies of scale.

It might matter less that national governments were remote, if authorities at a lower level were more accessible: there might still be local authorities, community or parish councils which were the prime source of loyalty and the prime agents of activity, and able to evoke the sense of community that is lacking within national states.

But in practice in most countries authority is passed ever upwards to larger and more unwieldy authorities, at county, regional or provincial level, that are ever more remote from ordinary people and their concerns. Genuinely local bodies, at the village or even borough level, no longer have any worthwhile powers which could allow them to act as a focus of sentiment. Those functions which they once undertook have been whisked away from them, and passed to still higher powers. The authorities still called 'local' today are far too remote, far too inaccessible to the average citizen, to appear to him as a close and benevolent, rather than as a distant and despotic power.

The sense of community is not *only* a function of size. It is possible to have a sense of community even among a large population if they are genuinely informed by common goals, as in a society in revolution or a nation at war for example. But it must inevitably be normally the case that the larger the numbers in a society the greater the proportion of total strangers, the wider the diversity of interests, views and concerns, and the harder therefore to create a sense of common purpose, still more a sense of neighbourliness. And undoubtedly modern cities, where most people today live, at least in developed and even in many developing countries, are inimical to community existence. Their sheer extent, the shape of the streets, the long rows of identical houses glaring across at each other, the vast blocks of indistinguishable flats, so close in physical distance yet so forbidding of social contact, the design of houses themselves, turned inwards, presenting barriers to the outside world rather than reaching towards neighbours, none of this conduces to feelings of community.

The socialist state has not solved these problems. Scale is no less. Cities are not smaller; nor their populations fewer. Systems of industrial organisation, local government structures, street plans and domestic architecture, are no different, no more community-minded. They reflect the norm of the industrialised world generally. The sense of community, which it was the primary aim of the early socialists to create, is no more visible there than elsewhere.

4 The Death of Diversity

4.1 *Modern Techniques of Socialisation*

The inexorable advance of large-scale organisation in general, and of state power in particular, has another effect. Besides destroying the sentiment of community, the increasingly complex and disciplined order which results leads in time to the destruction of *diversity*. It brings the elimination of the independent, the eccentric and the original; the imposition of a single, uniform, standardised system. This process too is to be seen in socialist and non-socialist systems alike. Indeed this too is perhaps most evident of all in socialist states.

Once again, it is the development of new means of communication which is the fundamental process at work. This not only makes possible the increasingly complex system of administration and organisation: it allows a more intensive socialisation process. The development of new mass media, the growth of new government techniques for public relations, the centralisation of organisation and administration, have the effect that the citizen is subject to more consistent pressures to conform with the patterns of organisation the society demands.

There are at root three separate processes at work. In modern societies more intensive, earlier, and longer education means that more detailed rules and instructions, covering a larger area of life and a larger number of responses and situations, are instilled: this conditioning brings increased *subordination* to prescribed roles. At the same time, more centralised, state-run education, a more unified mass culture-pattern, a nationalised communication system, reduce the degree of variation in the influences received by the child: this brings increased *standardisation* among the various available roles within each society. Finally, the larger scale of organisation, greater cultural uniformity both within and between societies, mean there is less variation between the norms established in different regions and countries: this produces increased *uniformity* in socialisation over large areas. Together they produce a more powerful, and more homogeneous process of socialisation than has existed in any earlier times.

The principal socialising influence in any society is language. This instructs us in the correct responses, emotions, gestures and attitudes for all stimuli and situations, establishes the basic social concepts, approved values and loyalties. In modern times, with the increase in the use of written language, its influence in instilling the prescribed attitudes and responses has probably become greater. But today local dialect and ways of speech decline, uniformity in language increases. A single, largely classless culture establishes a common language for all and so instils a common socialisation. Thus between states the increase in translation and interpretation, the transfer of terms from one language to another, the growing use of one or two world languages, mean that the variety of experiences and ideas that different languages previously provided is narrowed. To a large extent all become united, by a common linguistic background, in the veneration of the same worldwide concepts and beliefs.

More significantly perhaps, parental discipline and education become more uniform and consistent. From the baby's earliest years, approved methods of upbringing that will secure the production of 'well-adjusted' or 'normal' children are universally adopted. Dr Spock and his equivalents train parents in identical techniques, followed the world over. The age at which education begins becomes earlier, so the socialisation that results becomes more efficient. Education is more often public and state-controlled, which has the effect that there is more standardisation in methods and syllabuses; the eccentrics, who were self-taught, or trained, by cranky tutors or in cranky schools, into cranky attitudes, become fewer. The urge for equality causes all to be educated in the same classes, regardless of intellect or even interests, and to follow similar courses. Everywhere similar roles and attitudes become more firmly internalised, and the norms established increasingly difficult to resist.

Socialisation at later ages is affected similarly. The greater volume of social interaction tends to increase the degree of conformity both encouraged and demanded.[1] The proportion of people who live mainly solitary lives becomes far smaller. The peasant working alone on the land, the craftsman alone in his workshop, the hermit, the monk and the solitary scholar, each capable of insights and inspirations that were highly personal, and independent of general social pressures, disappear. They are replaced everywhere by the socially active town-dweller, working and living continually among large masses of people, and so increasingly dominated by the standards that prevail among them. Increasingly, all are conditioned by the wider society rather than the more intimate home or village.

More social intercourse and more entertainment reduce the proportion of leisure-time that is solitary rather than social. The off-time spent alone in the countryside, in the church, or even alone in the library or study, is increasingly replaced by off-time spent at the golf-club, the cocktail party, or in front of the television set, absorbing influences from society rather than from nature, from other people rather than other things. The demand, as well as the opportunity, for gregarious activity increases, as a relief from the emptiness of contemporary atomised and faithless societies. Intensive social activity provides a sense of belonging, a reassurance against anxiety and isolation, a mutual exchange of support or popularity, that can no longer be won in other ways. The cocktail party provides the maximum of gregariousness with the minimum of companionship. Even if genuinely social virtues, such as regard and consideration for others, are encouraged by this trend (which is doubtful), even that can entail a decline in spontaneity and individuality. The better 'adjusted' individuals become, the less of themselves remains. The more they adapt to the process of interaction, the larger becomes the part of their personalities which is borrowed from those they meet.

More powerful socialisation is effected also by more precise stereotyping of the norm demanded. The general concept of 'normality', in social intercourse and psychiatric practice alike, makes deviation everywhere a term of abuse or shame. The eccentric is renamed the 'abnormal', the original the 'neurotic', the unsocial the 'maladjusted'. Character-types and forms of behaviour once common become classified as 'unbalanced' and are treated out of existence: they are considered cured only when converted into the forms of behaviour approved as 'normal' (though the prevalence of mental instability and breakdown hardly suggests that modern society's demands are closely related to the demands of nature). Above all, because people are more self-conscious about their own personality-traits and behaviour than at any previous time, they become *themselves* more skilled in reshaping their own conduct into the socially accepted moulds. The co-operative, the responsive personality is encouraged. But because most goals are collectively rather than individually chosen, the habit of creative and self-originating desires declines.

More powerful socialisation even affects political attitudes. Modern means of education and mass communication media instil more uniform acceptance of the existing political system than in earlier times. Both populations themselves, and those who partici-pate in political life, are deeply conditioned by the already *established* procedures and institutional structure. Ruling parties and bureaucracies no longer seek or even wish for radical change. Even the young seek new ways of raising themselves through the existing system, not a new system altogether. The entire range of political discussion concerns whether there should be marginally more government intervention, or marginally less; marginally more public expenditure on welfare services or marginally less. Nobody challenges the whole system, still less the existence of the state itself. The state's own socialisation processes see to that.

Reaction against the brutality and injustices of authoritarian or competitive societies have undoubtedly brought, in socialist and non-socialist states alike, more cooperative and compassionate social and political systems. But the common goals of those systems, even if democratically chosen, increasingly impose their own built-in roles and attitudes. Eventually such a system may become a *perpetuum mobile* machine: in endless agitation, but never changing in its fundamental nature, nor departing significantly beyond the limits of movement laid down for it in advance.

4.2 *The uniformity of culture*

The development of improved communication-systems in modern states has another important effect; the diffusion of the approved political values, culture and way of life over wider and wider areas.

Within single societies, some standardisation of culture and values has always occurred. But modern communications have the effect that each society is far larger. This brings about cultural integration at an ever wider level. That process takes place both within and between states.

The most obvious visible sign is that *material* ways of life become more uniform all over the world. Until only the last fifty years there still existed huge varieties in culture, creed, costume, speech, customs, marriage laws and institutions among different peoples of different regions and continents. A vast range of wholly different cultures coexisted in various parts of the world, from Tibet to Tahiti, from Polynesia to Peru, Australasia to Arabia, Java to Japan. Already today these diverse cultures are everywhere diluted and dissolved, increasingly overlaid by the universal common norm imposed by modern industrial society. Not only are innumerable primitive societies, each with their own customs and beliefs – in Africa, in Asia, in Latin America and Australasia – eliminated or absorbed. Even developed civilisations and highly evolved cultures – in India, in Japan, in Iran and elsewhere – are increasingly assimilated to the common Western twentieth-century model. In every part of the world people lead similar lives, wear similar clothes, live in similar houses, read similar magazines, think similar thoughts. This is a total transformation of the world that has taken place, almost unnoticed, in only a few decades.

The diffusion of material culture, that formerly took hundreds or even thousands of years, today is almost instantaneous. So the latest industrial techniques, and the latest consumer goods, within a few years are spread all over the world. The spread of ideas, styles of art, beliefs, is only a little slower. Cultures not only spread more rapidly but rapidly become more and more alike. Styles of architecture, national costume, art and popular music, which were previously totally dissimilar among different peoples of the world, today become everywhere almost indistinguishable. In the Philippines as in West Europe, in Liberia as in Kuwait, in Bolivia as in the Soviet Union, men wear the same pin-stripe suits, drive in the same passenger cars, from similar blocks of flats, to identical office buildings, listen to similar pop music on identical radios. A single way of life increasingly envelops the world.

Within states too the variety once provided by cultural variety declines. Regional diversities of speech, language and custom become blurred or extinct. Differences between town and country are eroded, as the countryside demands to share the sophistication and amenities of the town. Art forms that once catered for possibly privileged, but at least diverse groups, or for religious organis-ations of varying faiths, are increasingly replaced by a common culture; folk art, national music and local dances of innumerable kinds and styles replaced by a universal mass entertainment and pop-music heard in every home simultaneously. Ideal homes, ideal heroes and heroines, ideal mothers and ideal babies, ideal hair-styles, ideal kitchens and ideal holidays, are projected into every household, and provide models that are universally emulated. What variety exists is obtained, not by catering for specialised groups or tastes, but by a rapid succession of tastes and trends that are each, for a moment, universally valid. Competition has the effect of confining styles to those acceptable to the largest possible number. So the consumer becomes finally influenced as much by the tastes of others as by his own. Records of the top ten acquire an instant sale *because* they are in the top ten.

There is also increasing uniformity between classes. Methods of baby care and child nurture become similar regardless of income, so that (though they may change rapidly with passing fashion) the children of each generation are everywhere produced upon a single jig. The relationships and methods of parents and teachers to children become standardised according to the prevailing principles. In education the desire for equality in standards and opportunities leads in practice, even if not in theory, to a growing identity in methods. Educational journals, ministry of education circulars, instructions in teacher-training colleges, the requirements of examinations and university entrance, all serve to bring about greater uniformity in the types of instruction everywhere afforded; and therefore in the type of knowledge, character and social norms instilled. Private instruction, whether by parents or tutors, which once produced a considerable proportion of the unusual minds and great intellects of the time; and self-instruction, which provided another common source of original and creative minds, today are both extinct. Education comes to be everywhere increasingly uniform.

Between nations too culture is increasingly standardised. Ideas and culture become internationalised. The same books, magazines, films, television personalities and social and political theories become known all over the world. The demand for equality, one of the most powerful motives that exists, promotes a demand for *similarity* (something quite different). Envy breeds imitation. Thus in most developing countries 'progress' is identified with assimilation of the thought patterns and way of life, the architecture, jazz, car-styling, films, clothes and household gadgets that are Western, or 'contemporary', in style. National and local traditions are despised as anachronisms. In religion, art and philosophy, the variety that formerly derived from regional and national diversity is replaced by a single monochrome international culture.

Even the dissident groups and movements become worldwide rather than local phenomena: hippies wear the same clothes, the same beads, the same beards, the same sandals and play the same music in San Francisco, Paris, Buenos Aires and Singapore. Political ideologies, social and sexual conventions alike become worldwide in their adoption. Monogamy and women's rights, for example, become world norms: and it is no longer possible for any society, however remote, however different in its own traditions, to claim (as a few years ago) that it prefers polygamy or male domination as part of its way of life. These are proscribed by norms that have now become universal in scope.

Nor can *individuals* ever escape these trends. The variety of occupation, culture and background that were once open to them is now closed. They can no longer choose, as their forerunners could only a century or two ago, to exchange the life and habits of an English gentleman for those of a Bedouin tribesman, those of a Venetian merchant for those of a Mongol official, those of a French stockbroker for those of a Polynesian villager, go from writer to peasant, or from pirate to monk. For if they go to the very furthest extremity of the globe, to the very opposite social pole or occupation from their own, they will still find waiting a culture and way of life barely distinguishable from that which they have abandoned. While technically existence as hermit or desert islander for the individual, or as pioneer community for the group, remains possible, physically, psychologically and sociologically they become increasingly impracticable. The hippy communes of New Mexico soon disintegrate and their once enterprising denizens drift back to the cities, to lead there precisely the same lives as their once-despised fathers and mothers undertook before them.

At root there are two trends at work. First, the common culture increasingly extends even to the remotest parts of the world, abolishing the diversity of culture-contacts and influences, the irruptions of new and alien styles, the variations, exceptions and freaks, that once stimulated new ideas and movements: so, even within the last twenty or thirty years, wholly unique cultures in Tibet and Lapland, Bali and Hokkaido have been overlaid and extinguished, destroyed by the common international twentieth-century 'civilisation' that has, with only small variations, replaced them. Secondly, the effect of increasingly powerful socialisation everywhere is that fewer and fewer even *want* to depart from the prevailing norm or to hazard an escape to some totally alien mode of existence. Increasingly all people everywhere wish to be like each other: or at least not too different.

4.3 *Uniformity of Values*

Even ethical ideas are affected by this process. Moral standards become increasingly alike, both between individuals of a single society and between cultures.

Between individuals, morality takes increasingly public rather than private form. The lack of privacy, and of challenges confronted in private, such as earlier ages have provided, reduces the need for privately evolved solutions and standards. The individual conscience tends to be replaced by social 'norms', or general consensus. More and more those acts are avoided that 'everybody' disapproves, rather than those that I personally disapprove. Between cultures, the contemporary communications system transmits the contemporary, common, science-based ethic, wholly displacing traditional, diverse myths and values. The division between faiths and moral systems, like that between social systems, thus becomes increasingly blurred and eroded.

The most important development is not simply that people become increasingly 'other-directed', ruled by the demands and values of others, rather than those they have themselves formulated; nor even that they internalise the values they are taught less perfectly, and therefore remain more insecure and subject to external influence (though both of these may be true). The more fundamental point concerns the nature of the values themselves. With better communications there is a perpetual convergence among the socialising agencies. Values become increasingly similar, increasingly consistent, and increasingly early instilled, so that there becomes less and less room for a variety of influences, or for personal choice, evolution or rejection at a later age. At the same time the habit of adopting personal, or absolute, standards is replaced by acceptance of those recommended by others, so that an instinct to conformity, a disposition to adopt the standards of the reference group or community, replaces personal standards internalised at an early age. In time therefore all standards everywhere become more and more alike.

This trend is even further promoted by prevailing psychological and moral attitudes, by greater recognition of the subjectivity of values. For the worthy belief in the duty to respect not merely the needs and views of others, but the value systems that underlie them, may promote the most fundamental conformity of all: behaviour that recognises the *standards* that others expect rather than those I expect myself. Where all practise this equally, all values ultimately become merged in a watery synthesis, representing the lowest common multiple of all. Social consciousness induces concern not only for what others want in a material sense, but for what others want in terms of values and ideals. And the ultimate effect may be that people become more concerned to do and say what others feel they should do and say than what they instinctively believe they should do and say: to be what others want them to be rather than what they are or want to be themselves.

Because the establishment of common standards today increasingly takes place at a world level, *conformity* more than ever before presupposes *uniformity*. Some pressures to conformity must always exist within all communities, small and large; but their effect becomes totally different when they occur throughout the entire area of human existence. This is the most important consequence of all of the establishment of a single international community. The culture-contacts and cross-influences that have in the past often formed the most fertile source of intellectual and cultural change become impossible. The only changes available are those that are internally evolved. In consequence social evolution itself, which in the past so often arose from external influences, may become increasingly marginal. The appearance of increasingly rapid social and political change may reveal itself as a situation of increasingly rapid progress towards increasing sameness everywhere.

4.4 *Order and Diversity*

The effect of the pressures of organisation in the modern world is thus both to crush community and to destroy diversity. Any attempt to re-humanise socialism, therefore, must take account of those dangers.

What we have examined reflects a primeval conflict of values. For thousands of years mankind has been attempting to reduce the suffering and discomforts of conflict and competition by establishing a greater measure of order within society. It has found the means of resolving the conflicts of families within a village, of villages within a region, of regions within a nation. It has found the means of organising economic activity in more complex ways by joining individuals together in workshop or in farm, by joining larger numbers together in factories, finally by organising world-wide industrial and commercial organisations employing tens of thousands of people. It has found the means of establishing services to relieve hardship and suffering, first in the village workhouse, then in city hospitals, finally in vast and elaborate health and social services covering an entire nation. It has found the means to coordinate transport, trade, monetary and other economic activities, first locally, then nationally, and now increasingly at the world level. It has found the means to establish greater equality through tax systems and welfare benefits. The creation of order out of chaos in almost every field of activity has been possibly man's supreme achievement: the way above all others in which human performance surpasses that of the animal.

But it is an achievement that has been accomplished only at considerable cost, a cost that is only now beginning to be visible. For order has been established only by inhibiting the capacity of man, individually or in groups, to create disorder, in other words by inhibiting his freedom and creativity. To establish an order, men have to be taught to fulfil roles, complementary or cooperative, on whose fulfilment the order depends. Indeed, eventually they are taught not only to fulfil those roles, but to recognise the categorical imperative that the fulfilment of each role is the essential condition of ensuring the fulfilment of corresponding roles by others: the condition of the order and stability they have been taught to cherish. Compliance in the role demanded then becomes, by that process, not compulsory but willing: the recognition of necessity.

This is an insuperable dilemma for society. Men can achieve greater freedom for themselves only by allowing the various orders, political, economic, social and legal, which they have established to disintegrate once more: only by once again allowing the strong to engage their strength at the expense of the weak. Yet in a world where justice, the protection of the weak against the depredations of the strong, has generally come to be demanded as the essential condition of most human arrangements – and where the weak are in any case usually in the majority – such relaxation of the orders already in existence is unlikely to be tolerated. So the process of increasing organisation will in all probability continue. But order and diversity, the establishment of stability and coordination on the one hand, and the capacity for individual men and groups to follow their own inclinations in pursuit of their own desires and values on the other, become increasingly difficult to reconcile.

There is only one solution, hard though it is, to this dilemma. The movement that has been set in motion, over many centuries, towards ever more complex systems of organisation in ever larger structures, has to be reversed. That implies that the large must be broken up into the small, and the complex organisation into the simpler organisation. For then, and only then, can men once more be at least partially released from the inexorable pressures which organisation imposes. Only in such circumstances will there at least be room for diversity between groups (if not always between individuals within groups). Then each group can pursue its own values, its own way of life, its own system of organisation. And men will be able as never before to *choose* their own group, their own type of society, their own way of life, according to their own values and aspirations, instead of according to the accident of where they were born.

Of course there will still be needed, if the world is not to revert to the chaos from which it has only slowly emerged, certain minimum rules of coexistence, a *modus vivendi* between the groups. But this does not necessarily entail the type of all-embracing, all-devouring, all-pervading structure which seems in danger of coming into being today. It does not even require the ever-present, and apparently indispensable, national state. Within the outer framework of basic rules a wide variety of independent communities or groups might live their separate lives, according to their separate value-systems. And socialism might be seen as a principle for organising individual communities rather than for building ever more centralised national states.

But such a reversal of the spiral can only come about as a result of a conscious and deliberate decision to bring it about, and to maintain it against all the pressures in the opposite direction. Such is the power of the downward-moving, the centralising, the organising forces, the forces that reduce societies and men into cogs within a single vast human machine, that increasingly impose an undifferentiated universal culture, that the simple *desire* for a return in the opposite direction will not be enough. To reverse the irreversible there will be needed a revolution in the most literal sense: a determination to unwind the machine, to set it going in the opposite direction, in other words to build a new kind of mechanism altogether.

For the first time there will have to be a desire to build downwards as well as up.

Part II Inequality in Modern World Society

5 The New Face of Inequality

5.1 *Traditional Political Attitudes to Equality*

A new approach to socialism will need first to reconsider one of socialism's most fundamental concerns: equality.

All political creeds have been concerned to establish a more 'just' society. A more just society need not necessarily imply a more equal society. The distribution of authority, status, wealth and influence regarded as 'just' will vary, for each individual and for each generation, according to deep-lying assumptions and preferences, deriving from basic value-systems and the guiding image of an ideal society. The relationships of a feudal society were 'just' to those who had been conditioned to feel that this was the *natural* order, or represented divine will. A society where all are precisely equal will be 'unjust' to those who believe it is wrong that ability and endeavour should go unrewarded.

Because of differences in these underlying value-judgements – in preconceptions concerning 'justice' – political thinkers have always shown ambivalence on the question of equality. Discussion of the subject has been bedevilled by confusion between 'is' and 'ought'; between equality as a 'natural', or previously-existing, condition among men, and equality as a state that should be *created* among them. Many of those believing the latter – who felt there *ought* to be a greater degree of equality in existing societies – have thought it necessary also to prove the former: that 'equality' *was* in some way the original, or natural condition of men, which had been destroyed by artificial, man-made social orders.

To some extent 'equality' as a natural condition has been accepted by all. All have accepted that men, however unequal in material conditions, are 'equal in the eyes of God', or 'equal in potential moral worth', or 'equal in their fundamental humanity' (a contention difficult to dispute). But from this assumption entirely contradictory conclusions could be drawn according to initial preconceptions or tastes: either that men should therefore logically enjoy equal rights on earth too; or that it did not matter how unequal their condition in this world, since God would anyway equalise them in the next.

It is possible to distinguish four main approaches among traditional writers, each representing a different use of the idea of 'natural' conditions. First, there have been those, such as Plato, who held men were naturally *unequal*, and therefore should be treated unequally in society. Those of superior wisdom or character should be the rulers; those with the souls of slaves should be slaves. This is the classic conservative view, which has been repeated in not very different terms throughout the ages. It assumes men are of a certain fixed 'nature', clever or stupid, industrious or lazy, good or bad, and once this nature has been established, they can be slotted, neatly and irrevocably, into the appropriate pigeon-hole. Since men are naturally unequal, whether in birth, talent or wisdom, they must be treated unequally. Attempts to treat them as equals would anyway be doomed to failure, since men will find their natural level. Moreover, to treat unequals equally is under this view as flagrant an injustice as to treat equals unequally. For Plato, the ideal of justice was 'to give every man his due', for each man to do his own work and not to interfere in that of others. Democracy thus militated against justice in according 'a sort of equality to equals and unequals'. Augustine declared that 'from Heaven to earth, from the visible to the invisible, some things are good, others better than others. In this they are unequal, so that all kinds of things might be.' Lamartine, in more recent times, declared it was impossible to reconcile 'the inequalities of virtues, of faculties, and of exertions, which distinguish men from one another' with equality of goods. In this view, hierarchy is a natural condition of men, and attempts to impose an unnatural equality will merely destroy excellence and individuality.

Secondly, there have been those who believed the exact reverse of this. Men are by nature 'equal', not of course in every respect, but in essential respects; and should therefore be treated as equals – again not in every respect but in essentials. This was the characteristic eighteenth-century view which was stated with varying nuances by many thinkers of that age to buttress the demand for a change in the existing highly unequal structure of society. Locke, Voltaire, Condorcet, Beaumarchais, Rousseau and others all expressed variations on this theme. So Locke declared that there was 'nothing more evident than that creatures of the same species and rank, promiscuously born to all the same advantages of nature and the use of the same faculties, should also be equal one amongst another without subordination or subjection.'[1] Rousseau spoke of the 'equality which nature has ordained among men, and the inequality which they have introduced'. And the framers of the American Declaration of Independence stated the view in its clearest and best-known form: 'All men were created equal and are endowed by their Creator with certain inalienable rights.' The exact sense in which men were 'created equal' was usually left veiled in discreet ambiguity. And this is understandable since, though it might be easily proved that in important respects men are essentially *alike*, it is difficult to show that in any respect they are exactly equal. Equality in 'rights' could perhaps be deduced, but on other grounds – the *likeness* among all human beings, or on grounds of convenience; but it cannot easily be deduced from a 'natural' equality which is itself difficult to discern. None the less, by these writers the original 'natural' equality is used to show the necessity of equality in political rights (Locke); in property rights (Condorcet, Rousseau); or in legal rights (Bentham). This necessity was by no means self-evident: the fact that men were *unequal* in certain respects – say intelligence, energy or wealth – might be held as relevant a reason for denying equal rights as the fact that they were *equal* in others – say humanity – was for granting them. The attempt to base a *desire* (men *should* be more equal) on an empirical statement (men *are* by nature equal) thus ran here into certain obvious logical difficulties.

Thirdly, there have been those who have taken the view that men *were* in origin equal, but should have the opportunity to make themselves unequal, through their own talents and endeavours. This is the extreme liberal view, characteristic of the second half of the nineteenth century. Here the belief is not so much in favour of 'natural' equality, though equality in starting-points is called for, but against *un*natural *in*equality. All the artificial impediments which create inequalities of *opportunity* – privileges of birth, inheritance and tradition – should be removed, and all should be allowed to find their own 'natural' level according to their own abilities. The fundamental concern here is with liberty, rather than equality. But this itself has implications for equality. For true liberty can only be achieved if all can feel they at least enjoy equal starting-points: these may then themselves be used to create further inequalities, but now earned rather than inherited. Here is introduced the dynamic element, the possibility of a change in status, which both our first views ignored. As one writer put it:

> The state gives equal rights and equal chances just because it does not mean to give anything else. It sets each man on his feet, and gives him leave to run.[2]

Herbert Spencer demanded 'equal freedom' under which 'every man may claim the fullest liberty to exercise his faculties compatible with the possession of like liberty by every other man': this principle of every man for himself and the devil take the hindmost might bring sufferings for some, but was held morally justifiable for was 'it not cruel to increase the sufferings of the better that the sufferings of the worse may be decreased?'

Finally, there was the fourth position: men are born unequal, whether by nature or economic circumstance, but they should be *made* equal by political institutions. Because some men are more skilful, ruthless, cunning, or simply more wealthy than others, in a totally free system there will emerge injustice, a system of exploitation of man by man. Men must, therefore do away with natural inequality by establishing a system in which men cooperate rather than compete, and can live in harmony under equal conditions. This is the socialist view, that began to be preached in the nineteenth century, and became more widespread in the twentieth. It is often combined with a historicist theory, according to which changes in the nature of society follow automatically from the inevitable forces of history or rules of economic development. Accordingly, to Saint-Simon, the old feudal society had established inequalities based on rank, wealth and status: but the new industrial society would establish a new principle of organisation by function, without domination: 'Each person enjoys a measure of importance and benefits proportionate to his capacity and his investment.' Marx declared: 'One man is superior to another physically or mentally. Equal right is an unequal right for unequal labour . . . It is therefore a right of inequality in its content, like every right.'[3] At root the distribution of goods is 'a consequence of the distribution of the conditions of production themselves' and this depended on the mode of production. Equality was not an end in itself: the abolition of inequalities might create as much envy and love of property as existed in the capitalist society: 'The vulgar Communist is only the consummation of this envy and this craving to level down.'[4] Only a total change in attitudes towards property could bring emancipation from its bondage, and the 'total freeing of all the human senses and attributes'. Similarly Engels in *Anti-Duhring* denounced the egalitarianism of his opponent and showed that 'every difference in the equality of the will, and in that of the intelligence associated with it, justifies an inequality of treatment which may go as far as subjection.' The bourgeois conception of equality failed to recognise that forms of equality and inequality are direct expressions of the system of production, and only a productive system in which the means of production were no longer in private hands could remedy the inequalities that at present existed. In other words, in an uncontrolled capitalist society inequalities would naturally appear. Equality could only be *created*, against natural forces, through the establishment of a wholly new type of society.

But even if thinkers accepted the need for a greater degree of equality among men, they still needed to decide what this meant. What kinds of equality ought men to enjoy? Locke declared that 'all men are by nature equal': but hastily added that by this he could not 'be supposed to understand all sorts of equality'. There were inevitably inequalities in age, virtue, merit and birth, but these were quite consistent 'with the equality which all men are in, in respect of jurisdiction or dominion one over another . . . that equal right which every man hath to his nature, freedom, without being subjected to the will or authority of any other man'.[5] Here the equality demanded was the political or legal equality in which none should enjoy a privileged position according them authority over others. Provided this was assured substantial inequalities in property were tolerable. But for others the reverse was the case. For Rousseau inequality in property was the prime concern, the most obvious fall from nature. Though born free, men were everywhere in chains precisely because of the inequality in property, and so in status, which men had introduced. But the restoration of equality required not only equal property rights but equal political power. 'From whatever side we approach our principle, we reach the same conclusion, that the social compact sets up among the citizens an equality of such a kind that they all bind themselves to observe the same conditions and should therefore enjoy the same right.'[6] Equality could only be restored by the establishment of a mutually agreed social order under the social contract.

An obvious question arose concerning the relationship between

political and material equality: which was the means to which?
Bentham restated the demand for equal political rights in terms of
an equal right to happiness: 'In proportion as inequality has place,
evil has place . . . the more remote from equality are the shares
possessed by individuals in the mass of the instruments of felicity,
the less is the sum of felicity produced by the sum of those same
shares.' An increase in equality in wealth must bring an increase in
total welfare, but this concern was for Bentham subordinate to that
with equal political rights. J. S. Mill, however, attached the
greater weight to material equality: 'No rational person will
maintain it to be abstractly just that a small minority of mankind
should be born to the enjoyment of all the external advantages that
life can give, without earning them by any merit, or by acquiring
them with any exertion of their own. . . While the immense
majority are condemned from birth to a life of never-ending,
never-intermitting toil.'[7] He thus held that: 'equality, though not
the sole end, is one of the ends of good social arrangements', and
any system which did not favour equalisation, 'whenever this could
be done without impairing the security of the property which is
the property and reward of personal exertion, is essentially a bad
government – government for the few to the detriment of the
many'. In Mill's view, however, this need for greater material
equality did not presuppose equality in political rights: here he was
prepared to accept, and indeed demand, considerable inequalities,
to take account of variations in wisdom and education.

Socialist writers had a clear view on this relationship. They
tended to hold, like Mill, that material inequalities were the more
fundamental. Once a more just material order had been established and private property abolished, political equality would
follow. According to Marx the socialist revolution, after destroying
the system of private property, would establish a dictatorship of the
proletariat, after which a socialist state would come into being, in
which political rights would be equally shared. He and other
socialists did not believe that political rights could be effectively
equalised, for example through an extension of the franchise, while
the system of private property remained.

The fact that some equalisation of influence and wealth through
precisely this process – the extension of the franchise – has in fact
occurred in Western societies does not remove the dilemma over
the relationship between different types of inequality. Material
inequalities have been somewhat lessened in the West following

the equalisation of political rights, even though a capitalist system of production has generally persisted; they have narrowed somewhat in the East under a socialist system of production while political inequalities have been wider than ever. But everywhere material inequalities remain wide. And it is clear that an apparent equalisation of political rights, whether in Western democratic states or in Socialist states, is not sufficient to secure the kind of equality within society that socialists have always demanded to see established.

5.2 *Material Inequalities*

Inequality has always been of many kinds: in political rights, in legal rights, in income, in property, in influence, in status, in opportunity, in education, and other assets. Much political writing of the past has concerned political rights, since this has seemed the most fundamental: once equality here was secured, it was felt, equality, or at least greater justice, in other fields would automatically follow.

In fact the experience of the last century has shown that, even after equality in voting rights has been achieved, it has had remarkably little effect on equality of other kinds: inequality in income, wealth and status remain today largely unaffected, in both socialist and non-socialist states. So it becomes necessary to look for other basic sources of inequality. Attention has shifted to inequality in education, inequality in status or inequality in influence as the basic sources of injustice. Yet important though these are, it can be held they are themselves only the effect of the more old-fashioned inequality in income. It is this material inequality which must still be considered the most basic and the most acutely felt.

In examining these material inequalities, it is important to consider first *where* they lie: to compare the relative income a head or standard of living of whole categories – for example between men and women; old and young; families with children and without; those with one kind of education and those with another; those in one part of a country and those in another. If socialism is concerned with inequality, it must be above all concerned with analysing between which groups the main inequalities exist at any one time. For in this way we may learn something of the causes of inequality, and how to remedy them.

Socialism must also be concerned with the *why* of inequalities:
the reasons used to justify them. Inequalities are often justified on
the basis of their effect as *incentives*, means of spurring men to more
effective action; or alternatively as *rewards* for special training or
responsibility. Thus it is necessary to consider how far is it true that
differences in income promote effort or initiative; or that they
correspond to differences in training, skill or responsibility.

Few people would deny that in some occupations payments by
results may act as important inducements, though there are also
countervailing disadvantages to set against them. If builders are
paid according to the number of bricks they lay, they will almost
certainly lay more bricks than if they are paid a flat rate. But they
may also lay more bricks wrongly. Piece-rates also lead to
innumerable disputes about rates and relativities and therefore
many stoppages. The net economic effect therefore is not necessarily advantageous. The fact that in many parts of manufacturing
industry today there has been a movement away from piece-work
towards time payments or other methods is an indication of the
disadvantages. Even, therefore, where methods of payment clearly
do act as some sort of incentive, they may be an incentive to the
wrong thing: to speed, rather than productivity. And there are
many occupations, clerical work, the civil service, transport,
teaching, most service industries and others, far more than half of
the total, where short-term incentives of this kind cannot play any
role because there is no easy way of measuring effort or success.

Similarly, the chance of promotion, also implying a form of
inequality, no doubt acts as a significant spur to some. But it is often
the status, rather than the money, won by promotion that acts as
the main spur. If increased status is the major incentive, this could
suggest there is a need for more promotion but with smaller
increases in pay in consequence. In existing industrial society most
working people can never be affected by this inducement at all,
since they can never expect to be promoted at all: on these grounds
there is a case for wider use of grading systems with incremental
scales throughout industry. Finally, it is important to be clear that
differences in pay *between different occupations*, which are the major
differentials, cannot act as an incentive to effort at all for most
people. Whatever the incentive case for a wide differential between
a good dustman and a bad one, an efficient director and an
inefficient one, it cannot justify the differential between dustmen
and directors generally. The dustman would need little incentive

to change places with the director; and indeed few people *require* inducements to secure positions of higher status and responsibility.

Even if it could be shown that monetary incentives were essential to induce adequate effort within particular occupations, it would still remain to be shown how great they need to be. In highly competitive societies, even quite small variations in levels of pay might act as a powerful motivating force; while conversely very large differentials can have a *disincentive* effect by causing discouragement and disillusion. In more relaxed societies wider differentials might be necessary. It is thus probably true that the more a society is 'achievement-orientated', as modern Western society is said to be, the *smaller* the differentials that are required as effective incentives. There is certainly no evidence at all that the differentials that at present exist in these societies bear any relationship to those that would be necessary to provide a set of scientific incentives. Incomes can be earned in some occupations several times the size of those to be earned in others where far greater effort and concentration is required. And at present the highest incomes of all are paid to those in occupations which in any case have the highest satisfaction of other kinds, both in the kind of work and the degree of status that they afford; and which therefore, on grounds of incentive alone, might demand the lowest rather than the highest rates of pay.

Thus the arguments traditionally put forward concerning incentives cannot be regarded as conclusive. Incentives clearly do have an effect on motivation, especially for particular types of worker. But they may also have many other indirect effects, which reduce rather than increase production. Many of the arguments used, though they cannot be dismissed as irrelevant, thus have much less weight than is normally accorded to them. And they all have to be set against the *social* disadvantages that may arise from very large differences in income.

Next, it may be held that a high income is required not as an incentive but as a just *reward*, for example for long or arduous training where this has been necessary. The doctor, it may be said, deserves to be well paid once he is qualified and well established in practice, as a reward for having to undergo several years of intensive study as a student, followed often by two or three years of hard and underpaid service as a house doctor in a hospital. This argument depends on certain assumptions (apart from the questionable assumption that hospital doctors are today underpaid). It seems to imply that the training period is unpleasant and must therefore be compensated for. Measurements of unpleasantness are always subjective and can never be firmly established. But certain tests are possible. Young men of seventeen might be asked whether they would prefer to spend the next eight years of their lives as medical students and house doctors or, for example, as unskilled factory workers, on the assumption that at the end of the period they would be paid the same and take up some other occupation altogether. On this basis it seems likely that the life of a medical student and house doctor under training would come high rather than low on the table of preferences. The assumed unpleasantness of study (an assumption that would anyway be challenged by many) must be taken together with the attractions of other aspects of the life of a student at a university or hospital. The same holds good of training for other highly-paid professions. It is rather the industrial apprentice who undergoes several years of training, at extremely low rates of pay, including arduous work and intensive study and inconvenience, with few of the attractions of the life of a student, who might more reasonably expect to be well rewarded at a later stage, in compensation for a spell of life considerably worse, both financially and otherwise, than many of his contemporaries who have already entered into highly paid employment can expect. Yet in this case the long-term reward obtained through such training is small and has been progressively reduced in recent years.

There does not indeed seem to be any clear logical reason in favour of granting rewards for training. It could even be argued that we should, more logically, pay more to the least educated in recompense for their *lack* of education, with all the advantages, opportunities and enjoyments that go with it, rather than pay more to those who enjoy both a more privileged existence in youth and a more priviliged occupation thereafter.

Much the same applies to the argument that the doctor deserves his high level of income, not as a reward for the *unpleasantness* of his training, but as a reward for the *skill* he acquires through it. If able students alone can acquire entry into a medical school, with many others weeded out during training, it is said, those who complete the difficult course and pass all the necessary examinations will be not only exceptionally able in themselves, but have acquired very special qualifications that require suitable reward. Again the logic of this argument is open to question. Whether native or acquired ability is concerned, the possession of skill is a privilege, not a hardship, and usually a pleasure to exercise, which may not require any other reward. Here the test would be to ask the doctor or the surgeon whether he would prefer to practise his own profession and skill, or to take up another, such as a factory worker's, if there were no difference in income. If they would prefer their own profession, this suggests that they require neither *reward* for practising it, nor *incentive* to do so. It is true that the skill of a doctor can be all-important in its consequences, and therefore highly valuable to society in a purely economic sense. But this is equally true of the skill of other specialists such as the engine-driver, the signalman, or the electrician, on each of whom life and death may depend, yet none of whom are particularly highly rewarded.

Besides, how should we make *comparisons* of skill? Is the skill of the motor-mechanic, or the watch-maker, or the cabinet-maker, acquired through years of experience and training, any less than that of the doctor – certainly of some doctors – or of the lawyer or the teacher? They are merely skills of different kinds. It cannot even be said that the skill of the doctor, or the professor, or the company manager, would never be acquired if there was no adequate reward to be obtained for it. On the contrary, the most highly paid occupations – those of the company director, the professor, the barrister, the airline pilot – are almost invariably also the most comfortable and enjoyable and the ones that would attract most applicants, regardless of the level of remuneration; while the jobs of the lowest paid, the dustman, the building labourer and the railwayman, are not only poorly paid but the most unpleasant and unattractive in themselves. Thus even the scarcity value of certain workers – say a professor, a manager or a surgeon – who have acquired certain skills is not in itself an argument for greater pay if they would come forward anyway for less. This would remain so even if there were no others who could do the job with the necessary training: which is in fact unlikely to be the case.

Thirdly, it may be held that certain occupations require an especially high level of reward because of the *responsibility* attached to them. Even if the doctor does not require special payment in reward for his training, or for the exercise of skill, he may need it in reward for the cares and worries he faces. It is no doubt true that there exist very real differences in the degree of psychological strain associated with particular occupations: because of the difficulty, or complexity, or importance of the decisions and actions to be taken. But it is not easy to compare this as between professions. Nor is it apparent that the highest rewards go where strain is highest. Pressures of responsibility are perhaps most intense among civil servants, and not only the senior ones, and among teachers; but it is doubtful if their pay reflects this at present. Again, the strain of working at pressure in very noisy conditions, on an assembly-line, is undoubtedly great but is scarcely reflected in pay for that work.

Nor is it self-evident that responsibility is always unpleasant to exercise, and therefore demanding of reward. The cabinet minister, and the company director, may indeed be highly conscious of the responsibilities they bear in reaching decisions they are called on to make. But it is not impossible that they enjoy, rather than dislike, that sense of responsibility. The railway signalman, worrying whether he has remembered to pull the right lever at the right time, or the teacher worrying about the progress of his pupils or the problems of maintaining discipline, the clerk worrying whether he has kept the accounts correctly, may *feel* as much responsibility over the exercise of their duties, and worry as compulsively, as the cabinet minister or company director about theirs. The fact is that the psychological burden created by responsibility will vary enormously from one individual to another, and it will be related rather to personality factors than to the nature of their duties; so that the reward to be paid in compensation could not be calculated on the basis of occupation alone. Finally, there is the problem of defining the causes of the psychological effects concerned. If the company director suffers from ulcers, is this always because of his sense of responsibility to his employees and shareholders, or because of worry about his own success and future income? Does the cabinet minister worry about his duty to his country, or about his personal career and prestige? So this argument too is certainly not a self-evident one.

Thus most of the arguments traditionally used to justify inequality in income are at least open to question. They tend frequently to be used as rationalisations to justify the level of differentials, the type of society, people wish to see for quite other reasons: because they suit their interests or correspond with their assumptions, aspirations or political beliefs.

The most important source of inequality is none of the rationalisations we have considered. It is convention. Socialist writers have traditionally demanded a greater measure of material equality than has existed in capitalist societies. And the removal of material inequalities of this kind has been regarded as a specially important aim of socialism. Yet in the socialist states that have actually been established (including semi-socialist states such as Britain), material inequalities are not significantly less than before. The range in incomes and way of life is almost unchanged. The strength of traditional differentials is so powerful that even when marginal adjustments are made the conventional relativities invariably return eventually.[9] And the arguments here discussed, concerning incentive, reward, skill and responsibility, flimsy in themselves, are rarely the decisive factors. It is tradition, *expectations* above all, that determine and preserve inequalities in income, in socialist as in capitalist states. Here too the establishment of state socialism has not brought anything like the transformation that has been expected of it.

5.3 *Non-Material Inequalities*

Moreover in modern society there emerge new forms of inequality which are no longer material at all. It is probably true to say that the disparities of which the citizens of today are most conscious are not primarily monetary but intangible; inequalities in status, influence, education, opportunities for promotion or change, conditions of work, social privileges and so on. In some cases these are partly the *result* of monetary inequalities. But they are not inherent in them. And often they have more important social effects than the monetary differences themselves.

One of the most important of these intangible inequalities is inequality in status. As material conditions improve beyond a minimum, so the citizen becomes less concerned about income or possessions, but more about his position within society, the respect accorded to him by his fellow-citizens, the credit he wins for (and from) his wife and family. Sometimes this is acquired as a *result* of material possessions, but this is not necessarily the case. Many with few possessions enjoy widespread respect; while conversely some who are extremely wealthy enjoy little.

Socialist theory has in general wished to see the creation of a society in which there existed no wide disparities in status. Under socialism 'class-consciousness' would decline, or disappear. A 'classless' society would be established.

It would be difficult to claim, however, that in the systems of state socialism so far established this has been the result. In such societies, as in the semi-socialist systems of the West, glaring differences in status persist. The dominance of large-scale organisations has the effect that there remain in those states – in state industries, in government departments, in large commercial organisations, above all in the party structure – many positions of high authority. The degree of respect demanded and accorded to those holding these positions is not significantly different in these 'socialist' states from that in others professing a different political philosophy. The establishment of a society where private property has been largely abolished has not had the effect, hoped for by many early socialist writers, that inequalities in status would be eliminated.

The same thing is true of the distribution of influence. This is another important form of non-material inequality. Early writers assumed that a socialist society, where property had been abolished, would be more fully 'democratic' than the capitalist states previously known. But, as has often been pointed out, capitalist states themselves have developed in a way that Marx and other socialists never anticipated or dreamed of. With the development of trade unions, of higher standards of living and education, and the universal adult franchise, the distribution of influence, like that of income, has become in the West somewhat more equal than a century or so ago. In 'socialist' states, as in East Europe, and even in China and Yugoslavia, on the other hand, influence remains highly concentrated among a relatively small and privileged section of the population. Far from becoming more 'democratic', they are more authoritarian in their system of government than most non-socialist systems. Even in semi-socialist states of West Europe influence is highly concentrated. Here again, therefore, the system of state socialism has failed to produce the results, in terms of reduced inequality, that many had hoped.

Perhaps the most important of the non-material inequalities is in education. In capitalist societies this often derives directly from inequalities in wealth: better education can be bought for money by richer parents. The immediate effect of this is of course that the inequalities of one generation are transmitted to to the next. One of the main features of this type of inequality is that it is outside the control of those mainly affected by it: that is, the children whom it divides. Their ability to enjoy a particular kind of education is unrelated both to their own efforts and their own capacities. It is not unreasonable to argue that entry to schools is a question that should be determined on educational grounds, and not on extrinsic factors unrelated to scholastic ability. This objection will be particularly strong if the non-educational criteria have important social effects, in addition to their educational ones: such as the perpetuation of a particular class structure, and the segregation of children on class lines at the most formative stage of their lives. Other considerations are the need to ensure that scarce educational facilities are enjoyed by those best able to benefit from them, and the difficulty created for an effective public system of education while there remains a private system, taking a varying number of children, sometimes including the most gifted, out of the system altogether.

It is thus not unreasonable to conclude that the need to preserve the 'right' of parents to buy what education they like for their children is a less compelling argument than is sometimes suggested. Many would hold there exists a more important right: that of *children* to enjoy an equal start in life with each other, a right which is incompatible with the former. An equal start could still be reconciled with giving parents the maximum possible choice of *school*, of the most varied character and method though of equal standard, within the public system. The final choice of pupil would remain with the school and would be exercised in the interests of the pupils alone, on criteria related to their own abilities and interests.

In socialist societies, educational selection is not undertaken on the basis of means. But it can scarcely be said that inequalities in education have been abolished in such societies either. In the Soviet Union and China the intellectually gifted are given access to a wholly segregated system of schooling, specially designed for the intellectual elite. Such segregation must inevitably establish, even in the school years, a form of class structure, even if based on intellectual capacities rather than income (this too will transmit, only marginally less than a fee-paying system, class differences from one generation to the next). Moreover there exist usually, in both types of society, substantial differences in the length of education, which finishes for some at 16, for some at 18 and others at 21 or even later. Though these differences too are usually based on intellectual capacity, they none the less have the effect of radically affecting the opportunities available to those receiving different educations for the rest of their lives. Since it is extremely difficult for educational qualifications to be attained at any later age, to a considerable extent the fortunes which are available to individuals are determined by examination performance during four or five years of their lives.

Another major form of non-monetary inequality is the difference in the opportunities for job-satisfaction available to people in the course of their working lives. There are not merely very big variations between different occupations or organisations, but there are very large differences even within the same organisation, especially between wage-earners and salary-earners. These may relate to length of notice of dismissal, length of holidays, sickness allowance and treatment, pensions, the use of cars and other perks, eating facilities, and many others. Perhaps most important are the provisions for 'allowances', often very substantial and usually tax-free, and other forms of payment made in kind, housing, holidays, school fees, share distributions to executives, and large gratuities made on retirement.[8] Taken together these various forms of benefit may bring about differences in living standards that are considerably more significant than those that exist in levels of pay.

Another important form of non-monetary inequality is that which occurs in the field of law. The fact that in most Western societies enormous sums are paid for the services of the most gifted advocates is *prima facie* evidence that their employment can affect the outcome of a case; and, therefore, that those who can afford to obtain them secure a legal advantage over those who cannot. This most conspicuously affects civil suits. Those without financial backing not only have less gifted advocates. Because they may be unable to face even the *possibility* of having to pay heavy costs, the less wealthy citizen, unable to secure legal aid, may often be forced to withdraw from cases they have a reasonable chance of winning. In particular, large firms, easily able to afford legal fees, or employing their own lawyers, have a substantial legal advantage over small firms and the ordinary citizen. But the same factor can even affect criminal cases: a wealthy person may have a greater chance of securing acquittal in a marginal case by instructing the most expensive advocate, on a charge on which another might have been convicted. Legal aid systems do not overcome this problem, both because only those of very low income are helped by them, and because the most gifted advocates do not work for them. This suggests that if any real equality before the law is to be assured, it is necessary for the services of all advocates to be equally available, rather than sold at will to the highest bidder. This could only be achieved if they were to become employees of the courts, choosing their briefs on the merits of the case rather than the size of the fee.[10]

These are only a few examples of some of the more conspicuous types of non-material inequality which exist today. It is probable that non-monetary inequalities of this kind may come to appear increasingly important in relation to those of wealth itself. There is little evidence that most of the types of inequality, any more than inequality in income, are less apparent in the socialist societies so far known, than they were in earlier societies. But if it is one of the objects of socialism to do away with inequality, socialism must be concerned about inequalities of this less tangible kind, as well as those which are reflected in income.

5.4 *Collective Inequalities*

There is, however, another change in the nature of inequality in the modern world which is even more important in its effect on traditional socialist theory.

For one of the major effects of large-scale organisation today is that the most important forms of inequality are no longer individual but collective. Increasingly, as we saw earlier, the welfare, the opportunities, and the standard of living of each individual are determined, not by his own activity but by the activity of the group or organisation to which he belongs, and the services and amenities it provides: the economic enterprise, the region, above all the nation. Thus the success that is important to his welfare is not his own, or even that of his family, but that of his community, enterprise, or state.

In modern societies – both in capitalist and in socialist societies – it is collectivities rather than individuals that primarily save, accumulate and multiply wealth. According to their success in doing so, the fortunes of their members or employees vary widely.

The comparative success of the *enterprise*, capitalist or socialist, affects employees in many different ways. In the most immediate sense it affects the conditions in which they work. The successful enterprise provides palatial offices, glamorous secretaries and wall-to-wall carpets, as against the simple or tumbledown work-place of the small and struggling enterprise. The successful enterprise will provide lavish out-of-work amenities for their employees in the form of clubs, welfare outings, sports facilities and much else; while the unsuccessful firm may be able to provide nothing at all of this kind. Even on the shop-floor conditions may vary widely according to how far the enterprise can provide the most up-to-date buildings, equipment, canteens and other facilities. But, more significant, with increasing decentralisation of bargaining, the successful enterprise (in socialist as well as Western states) will often also provide higher pay. This is true especially for the increasingly numerous salaried class, whose incomes are individually negotiated. But, with rates of pay now separately bargained in each enterprise, it often affects other workers as much. The successful, and especially the larger, enterprise may pay more for exactly similar work. Equally important, the successful enterprise will provide generous pension funds, financed partly out of profits. It provides for executives' savings schemes, educational grants, golden handshakes and other fringe benefits which the small firm cannot offer. On the other hand, the unsuccessful firm may provide not only lower pay and unsatisfactory working conditions, but perhaps short-time work, finally total redundancy. Pensions and sickness benefit will be lower than in the successful firm. With the increasing concentration of industry, and the less perfect competition that accompanies it, these differences between the large and successful and the small and struggling firm probably become greater rather than smaller; and create greater inequalities between individuals in their way of life.

More important in their effect on individuals are inequalities between *regions*. Here too individuals acquire a big pay-off, or pay a heavy penalty, according to the degree of development, or success, of their own region. In its most obvious and acute form, this collective inequality is seen in the different availability of employment opportunities in different regions. Usually there is a persistently higher rate of unemployment in less developed regions than in others. Wage-rates are frequently lower. Social services, the standard of roads and buildings, entertainment and the arts, are worse. Prices are sometimes higher, especially if the region is remote. Regional policies by governments to overcome the inequalities are usually only marginal in effect. The disadvantages can of course be off-set by bodily removal elsewhere. But this cannot be undertaken without considerable cost to the individual and his family; and the regional differences for those remaining may then become even worse.

This inequality shows perhaps most clearly in the differing revenues of different regions, according to the degree of development, which in turn affect standards of social and other services, and above all different standards of cultural life and so on. The physical environment of the more prosperous areas is incomparably superior to that of declining regions. These not only have old fashioned offices, shops, housing and other buildings, because of their failure to attract new industry; even their highways, their libraries and their public parks are likely to be inferior. Private and public squalor (like private and public affluence) go together rather than the reverse. Thus the individual's whole environment, socially provided, is an increasingly important part of total welfare.

The importance of regional differences is not significantly different under state socialism. In the Soviet Union or Yugoslavia, each with a number of republics, the differences between the Russian and Uzbek republics, between Croatia and Montenegro, is as clearly visible as in Italy, where the south remains perennially depressed, or Britain, where the north does. This affects the attitude of each region to economic reforms aiming at decentralisation: the richer republics of Yugoslavia, like oil-rich Scotland in Britain, want more local control while the less developed oppose this.

Private investment has the same disequalising effect. A large proportion of private investment naturally goes mainly into existing plants in the regions already most prosperous. Even the private capital that does move goes predominantly into the most developed areas, where there exist skilled labour forces, good communications facilities, specialised services, above all the mass markets, which make such investment profitable. So more developed states of the United States, such as Texas and California, become still richer while Mississippi and Alabama remain always poorer. Against these natural economic pressures, even the most massive regional programmes of governments find it difficult to make headway.

But by far the most important type of collective inequality today is that between different *nations*. For nations are today the primary instruments for the accumulation and investment of wealth. Although this wealth derives originally from individuals, it is appropriated by their governments for national purposes. It is used partly in activities undertaken directly by governments: in administration, social services and nationalised industry – together often taking half the national income. The welfare of individuals depends largely on these collective actions and policies: in other words, on which state they belong to.

But the citizen benefits not only directly from government action, but indirectly, from the wealth of his state and all that results from this. The richest states, because of their greater investment rates, monopolise a greater and greater part of the world's income. Because they can use advanced technology not available to the less developed (and because primary products and simple manufacturers represent an even smaller proportion of consumption), they increase their share in world trade. Even if rates of growth and population increase were equal all over the world, the gap between the richer and poorer nations would increase all the time, by a process of compound interest because in *absolute* terms their increase in wealth is much greater. And since rates of population growth are higher in the less developed, in fact the inequalities in income, and so in welfare, increase even faster. Today, therefore, by far the most important inequalities that exist are those between states, not within them.

Even if within states personal incomes were becoming more equal therefore (which is true in only a few countries), they are often overtaken by new inequalities that are collective rather than personal in form. One reason why collective inequalities have become today so much more important than individual inequalities is that the process of inheritance (the prime source of inequality among individuals in the past) is today far more important among these collective units than it is among individuals. The inheritance of individuals from their families, whether of cash or of property, can be, and is, severely limited by governments, through capital transfer taxes, death duties and other measures. But the inheritance by firms, regions and nations of capital assets inherited from the past is unconditional. This is so especially in the last case. For the assets of firms and regions may be taxed to some extent by the state itself. But those of the state are inalienable. And as a result the inequalities between states, each increasing their wealth according to their own capabilities, become greater all the time.

Thus while among individuals the *hereditary* class-system, ossifying the distribution of wealth from one generation to the next, is partly disappearing, through the working of the tax system and other factors, among collectivities wealth remains even more clearly divided between economic classes: between haves and have-nots. Among states indeed, the dividing-line can be far more clearly seen than class divisions ever could. Living standards change sharply at the frontiers: between the US and Mexico, South Africa and Lesotho, the Soviet Union and Afghanistan. To a considerable extent today individuals are as rich as the community in which they live. At the very moment when inequalities among individuals within states – the material ones at least – are beginning to be marginally reduced, inequalities between states become greater all the time.

If equality remains a central concern of socialism, therefore, it must today be above all the removal of *collective inequalities*, especially inequalities between states, that it should seek. But state socialism of the traditional type can be of no assistance here. For under that system it is the state itself that accumulates wealth. By definition it can bring about no transfer of resources between states. To remedy the worst inequality of the modern world therefore a new and different form of socialism may be required.

6 Inequality in Political Influence

6.1 *The Theory of Democracy*

Socialists were originally, like other political thinkers, especially concerned about the just distribution of political power. It was widely felt that a greater equality in this sphere would lead in time to greater equality of other kinds. Once the state had fallen into the hands of the people, whether by revolution, as many felt inevitable, or by other means, a wholly new system would come into being, under which political influence would be permanently more widely distributed. The mass of the people would control the state and would determine the decisions and policies which swayed their lives.

Thus, though not all democrats were socialists – many wanted to see a broadening of the franchise and other reforms who never favoured the establishment of a socialist state – most socialists regarded themselves as democrats: they believed that the abolition of the private ownership of property, and its replacement by social ownership, would bring about a fairer distribution of political as well as economic rights within the state.

A number of arguments have been used to justify the modern democratic system:

Absolute power, it has been held, whether for a single ruler, a small oligarchy, or a whole class, will always ultimately corrupt and be used for selfish purposes: only a system that makes government responsible to all will therefore prevent such abuses of power.[1]

Rule by a government that is totally beyond control, whether tyrannical or enlightened, will create an intense sense of frustration and grievance for its citizens: it is thus necessary to provide *consent* in the acts of government, and ultimate redress in the form of the right to dismiss an unsatisfactory set of rulers through elections.[2]

All men are likely to be better judges of their own interests than even the most enlightened of their fellow-citizens can be (or at least will feel themselves to be so): only if all can equally promote their interests through the machinery of the democratic state, therefore, will all interests be equally protected.[3]

There will always be strong differences of view and of interest among the members of every state: a system of government in which everybody shares will resolve such conflicts more peacefully and justly than the more violent and more arbitrary method of solving them on the basis of power that otherwise results.[4]

Because, under a democratic system, political parties are obliged to compete for popular support throughout the electorate, they are likely to advocate and implement the policies that will most satisfy the greatest number of the electorate.[5]

Many heads are better than one: collective decisions, reached through the processes of consultation and discussion within a democratic state, are thus likely to be wiser, or at least less irresponsible, than decisions reached through the unfettered discretion of a single autocrat, or even a small oligarchy.[6]

Because other forms of influence over government are likely to be unevenly distributed, the influence provided through a franchise distributed among all adult inhabitants, each equipped with an equal right to choose his rulers, will go some way to nullifying these inequalities.[7]

Finally, participation in public policy is the basic right and duty of the educated and responsible citizen: the democratic system is thus necessary for individual fulfilment, as much as for social stability, justice or efficient government.[8]

These are, briefly summarised, probably the most important arguments that have been used to justify the democratic system as it is correctly practised. They are not wholly consistent with one another. Some advocate the democratic system because it is the most *acceptable* form of government; others because it is the most *just*; others as the most *peaceful*; and others as the most *efficient*. Some demand it for the sake of society – to provide stability, peace or progress; some for the individual citizen – to provide participation, influence or freedom from oppression. But it is not necessarily the case that all these aims can equally be attained by any one system. It is perhaps even more unlikely that *all* are best fulfilled by that system today known as the 'democratic'.

In some of the arguments described, moreover, the conclusions do not follow automatically from the premises. The fact that many heads are better than one is an argument against autocracy, but not necessarily for democracy as generally understood today. The fact that participation in policy-making is desirable does not show that parliamentary democracy can provide it. The fact that each man can best judge his own interests (even if true) does not prove he *can* protect them effectively under democracy. In some cases the premises themselves are questionable: are men always the best judges of their own interests, does power always corrupt? Even if both premises and conclusions were accepted, it is not proved that the purposes stated could not be still better attained by other means: can a representative government, or widely-based control over government policy, really be best achieved by the present parliamentary system? Finally, there may be further purposes that are relevant, which this set of arguments ignores altogether: the need for the protection of group interests and minority views, rather than of majority opinions only; the need for social or technical progress; the need for expertise in the business of government; the need for popular influence over individual decisions as well as over the choice of rulers; and so on.

Besides, even if one accepted the arguments, and so the need for some system of 'democracy', what exactly does that word imply? For the concept is one, like many of those employed in political discussion, capable of a wide range of meaning. Western and Communist states alike, for example, claim the name for their own system, and deny it to the other. The latter lay emphasis on equal economic rights and opportunities, democratically shared property, and political control by a 'democratic' party, representative of the working classes as a whole. The former use the word to describe a system of regular elections, usually within a multi-party system, in which a choice of governments is available under conditions of free speech and a free press.

But even among Western societies the content of the word is highly ambiguous. Clearly in derivation it implies 'government by the people'. But what is meant by that? Is a wholly autocratic government, but with popular referenda on all the main issues of policy, more or less 'democratic' than one with a parliamentary system, but with no choice by the electorate over the parties' policies? Is a one-party state with genuinely free voting for its members of parliament more or less 'democratic' than a multi-party state with strict whipping (as today in Britain)? Is a system with only independent members and no party discipline more or less 'democratic' than one with national political pro- grammes for each party, to which all candidates are committed, so that electors can know which policies will be pursued? Is a government that is totally indifferent to all public opinion and influence *between* elections, but submits itself for re-election regularly, more or less 'democratic' than one which is highly responsive to public opinion on all issues but retains power indefinitely? Is a government that is *composed* of members of the mass of the working class more or less 'democratic' than one *elected* by them? Is the regular election of a single leader to form his own government 'democracy'? Can one have democracy without parties? Or without parliament (but with an elected government)? Or without elections (but with referenda)? There would be little agreement on any of these points, though all of them are basic to the meaning of democracy.

In Western usage, in defining a country as 'democratic' we imply the existence of parties and of regular elections. The implication is, too, that there is universal, or nearly universal, adult suffrage; that elections are held under conditions of freedom of speech, of press and of assembly; that parties contesting the elections give some clear indication of the policies they will pursue if they are elected; and that the governments elected submit themselves to some questioning and probing by an elected parliament between elections, and are at least in theory responsible to parliament. Whether this sytem can fulfil the essential aims of a democratic system depends what one regards as the main object of the system: a check on the executive; the representation of personal or sectional interests; the control of legislation by a representative body; the right of the people, or of its representatives, to dismiss a government; the control of the state by the largest single class; the need to provide the citizen with a sense of control over his destiny; or the need to secure an equal, or at least fair, distribution of influence. These are each quite separate aims, requiring perhaps quite different institutions. And there is surprisingly little dis- cussion in modern 'democracies' of what institutions or arrang- ments are required to secure each of them.

6.2 *The Democratic System in Conditions of Large-scale Organisation*

The heart of the democratic idea for many is the desire that every citizen, however humble, should be provided with some sense of control over his own destiny, some ability to influence the decisions that most closely affect him. There are a number of reasons why, under modern conditions of large-scale organisation, the 'democratic' system fails to provide any real sense of control by citizens of their fate of this kind.

One of these is the factor we have already discussed: the sheer scale of modern societies. Administration often appears too remote for any effective control by the electorate, or even by their representatives. Because of the size of the political unit the top administrators, even at local government level, are not known, and rarely even seen, by the citizen. Still less is his MP, or even his borough councillor. For this reason alone it is extremely difficult for him to influence decisions. Decisions seem to be reached by unknown individuals, very far away, usually behind closed doors. Not only ministers and civil servants but the local planner, pensions official or housing manager may appear remote, obstinate, and deaf to complaint. They may seem tied by bureaucratic rules; or they blandly reassert that official policy must be right because it is official policy. The man in the street then feels impotent and frustrated: even if patient and reasonable (which they are not always), the powers that be seem impervious and beyond control. Thus, paradoxically, authority today often seems in some ways even more immune to influence than the power exerted by wholly authoritarian states in earlier times. The emperor of old, though wielding absolute power, might personally listen to the individual petitioner and redress his grievances instantaneously. Today the citizen with a grievance may have difficulty even in finding the responsible authority, let alone in making himself heard. However many votes he casts, the citizen thus feels little sense of control over the way he is ruled, still less participation in it. Government appears external, an outside force that must be accepted, not shared or controlled. The man in the street becomes increasingly conditioned into accepting what 'they', the authorities, choose to decide for him.

Secondly, in contemporary democratic states the electorate, while it can elect its government, possesses, even in theory no control over the *policies* of that government: which is what most matters to it. It is not even consulted about the individual measures which a government introduces. It is not even given a chance to pronounce on a *package* of policies, independently of choosing a government. It is allowed only the opportunity, once every few years, to choose between different sets of governors. Though these will often be closely associated with a particular set of policies, and may present themselves to the electorate on that basis, this gives little real choice to the elector. An elector may prefer one team as the potential government (on general grounds of administrative capacity, leadership, experience, or other personal qualities), but disapprove of each of the policies it presents at a particular election. More often, he will approve some measures in one party's programme, some in the other's. Even if a government were elected on grounds of policy alone (which is not the case), and if it were elected to power with five main planks of policy, therefore, each of those planks might be approved by only one-tenth of the electorate, voting for it on that issue alone: as a result the government might obtain the 50 per cent of votes necessary for election and be elected, on policy grounds alone, to implement a programme each and every item of which was rejected by nine-tenths of the population. This is an extreme hypothesis. But a government may well be elected because of general confidence in its capacities, not because of its policies: at most one or two policies may be widely approved by the electorate, while others are widely condemned. A government will still then represent itself to have a 'mandate' to implement *all* its policies, approved and disapproved alike. Often, electors do not even *know* well what policies a party advocates. If there are many parties, with each party representing a more narrow interest or programme, a rather more specific choice of policy is offered to the elector, but less chance of it being fulfilled: the programme finally implemented is likely to be rather the outcome of prolonged bargaining between the coalition parties, and may in no way reflect the views of the electors as a whole. Conversely, if there are only two parties, there may be no party that closely reflects the opinions of most electors. If democracy is taken to imply the implementation of policies approved by the majority of the electorate, therefore, it is certainly not fulfilled in modern democracies.

Thirdly, the electorate can only influence policies, even in this indirect sense, *after* they have already been adopted. It has no influence on the initial choice offered. It is given the choice between two lengthy and elaborately prepared programmes only when these have been fully debated and decided elsewhere. In practice it is not so much in the election that the important decisions are taken, therefore, but in the determination beforehand of what proposals are to be *presented* to the electorate. This decision may be made by delegates at a party conference; by the party machine; usually by a small clique within the party leadership immediately before an election. Yet this, the *choice* of policies, is the absolutely crucial decision. A handful of people within one party making that decision count for much more in determining the country's future than the government, the legislature or the electorate as a whole. Thus democracy in the sense of *choice* by the people of the policies to be pursued by the government is also not afforded under the current system.

Fourthly, even the limited choice offered by elections occurs only at rare intervals, usually between two and five years apart. Yet many of the most important decisions to be made may not have been anticipated in advance and could not have been. Thus a government has to take a large number of immediate decisions without reference to the electorate. Most of the decisions actually taken by governments are neither referred to the electorate directly, nor form any part of the political programme on which the government fought the election. Most of the important decisions reached in Britain in the last two decades (for example, the introduction of planning machinery by the Conservatives in the early sixties, their introduction of legislation against resale price maintenance, their application for membership of the European Community, the similar decision on Europe by the Labour Government, the Labour Government's introduction of statutory wages policy, its decisions on immigration, nuclear policy, East of Suez, and proposals in trade union law, the total reversal of economic policy by the Heath government and the adoption of a new statutory incomes policy, the similar decision on incomes policy by their Labour successors in 1975) were unmentioned in any party manifestoes. Theoretically the electorate still has the chance to pronounce a verdict *ex post facto* on the policies of a dying government at the next election. But this is irrelevant: it is by then too late. The new innovation in policy has been introduced (and in practice the result of the election will then depend not on approval of the innovations but on the state of the economy at the time). To a very considerable extent, therefore, a government possesses complete freedom of action on the vast majority of issues that arise. Thus even democracy in the limited sense of *endorsement* of government policies is not provided.

Fifth, even the people's 'representatives' in parliament exert no more effective control over the government in most such systems than the electorate. Instead of controlling the government, the legislature (the majority in which is bound to the executive by close ties of loyalty and interest) is itself normally controlled by it. The role of watchdog over the executive is thus played by a running-dog of the executive, obedient to its lightest word. While some reverse influence by the executive over the legislature is the condition of effective government (a condition often not fulfilled in the US), the domination it enjoys in most democratic states today has removed all meaningful power from parliament altogether. In any case the main influence exerted over the MP is not that of his constituents, nor of the voters that elect him, but that of the party whip, or occasionally of his local party caucus. Both of these are more likely to penalise him for exercising any individual judgement (whether or not this conforms to the will of his constituents) than to encourage him to do so. As a result, no government today, in Britain or most other democratic states, is ever seriously threatened by parliament, and virtually no government action or legislation is ever rejected (the US is here an exception). This may have its advantages. But it means that a government is no more responsible to the legislature than it is to the electorate. In 'democratic' states and in one-party states alike, government is in practice virtually under the control of an oligarchy of party leaders. Even that highly restricted form of democracy, *parliamentary* control of the government, is thus not provided under the system.

Sixth, many of the most important decisions are in any case taken outside parliament. Economic planning boards, incomes commissions, regional planners and other authorities, the boards of nationalised industries and private companies, all of these take decisions that affect the man in the street quite as closely as those of parliament itself. Yet these are responsible to nobody. Economic decisions, in state and private industry alike, are taken by small groups of people, wholly beyond the influence of any representative body. Social service agencies function largely independently, yet their decisions affect individuals vitally. Countless committees operate behind the scenes, taking many vital decisions almost unknown. As government becomes more complex the number of bureaucratic decisions, as we saw in Chapter 2, perpetually increases. Even some bodies that are in theory representative - hospital boards, police committees, housing committees - in practice often meet in private, and become as remote from the public as the bureaucracies. Not only government decisions, but many others equally vital to the citizen, appear to him to be reached without reference to his views. Democracy in the sense of government by *consent* is also not fulfilled therefore, since consent is not normally even asked for.

Seventh, decisions are influenced by other means, often far more effective than the use of the vote. Pressure-groups, skilled in the techniques of influence, often exert more sway on government decisions than voters, party members or MPs. Public relations and advertising techniques are used to promote a particular policy or viewpoint. Because such methods are increasingly common, those wishing to influence governments increasingly organise themselves in this way, rather than trying to influence parliament. In many cases they have their own private access to ministers and officials. The relative influence so acquired by each group often bears no relation to the numbers who support them within the electorate as a whole. Some groups (such as farmers or the directors of large economic enterprises) may be far better organised to ensure that their views are heard than others (such as housewives, pensioners or the small shopkeeper). Television, newspapers and other media may be more open to one group than another. Particular advisers, groups, or even departments within the government, may acquire an influence out of all proportion to the opinions or interests they represent. The balance among views and interests within the electorate as a whole may then be overturned by the differential capacity for influence enjoyed by particular groups. Thus if democracy is taken to mean equal representation of interests, this too is not fulfilled in complex modern states under the current democratic system.

Finally, another effect of large-scale organisation is that the relevance and meaning of 'democracy' is affected by the emergence of a single world political community. In the new international society, even if effective public control over *one* government could be obtained, this is less and less significant. When communications, trade, investment, travel, financial policy and military security overflow from one nation to another as today the destinies of individuals are affected by the decisions of international bodies more than of national; and by decisions reached in *other* states as much as by those in their own. When the power and wealth of some countries so enormously exceeds that of others, however democratic the institutions of single states, they may provide their citizens with little control over the events and decisions that affect them most: those made by their powerful neighbours. International organisations and international companies undertake activities and reach decisions which may affect the citizen quite as much as those of his government. In small nations and weak nations, particularly, even if their own system provides citizens with some influence in government, this will not influence these powerful, transnational forces. In other words the size and scale of the activities that most influence the life of individuals and states now transcend that of the dominant political institution, the nation-state: only democracy within the wider world could today secure, for most people, a greater sense of control over their destiny.

In contemporary conditions of large-scale organisation, therefore, the citizen feels lost, too insignificant to exert any effective influence. And this feeling of being without effective control over the decisions that affect him, of being in many ways *more* dependent than the citizen in earlier times, is no different in socialist societies: in the socialist states so far established the ability of the citizen to influence the decisions of government is indeed far less than in the West. State socialism as practised today, far from leading automatically to a more democratic style of government, has had the opposite effect. If socialism is concerned to provide greater equality, not only in a material sense, but in influence within society, then better ways of affecting this than those so far employed either in democratic or communist states today are required.

6.3 *The distribution of influence*

The reason that the modern democratic system – the right to vote every few years – has not seemed to give the average citizen today any effective say in the way he is governed, to provide any genuine 'democracy', is that it does not ensure that in any *individual* decision any account will be taken of the majority's wishes. They can choose the government but not what it does. What that citizen therefore demands, above all, is the right, if not to control, at least to *influence*, the individual decisions that determine his existence. Socialists who wish to see a more democratic system of government must therefore be above all concerned with a more just distribution of influence within society.

It cannot be said that at present, either in socialist or non-socialist states, influence is evenly distributed.

All men possess some influence. Even in highly organised societies, though authority is remote, influence is to some extent shared: the influence of the production manager is balanced by that of the sales manager; that of the general secretary of a union by his executive committee; that of the minister by the cabinet committee; that of the government by the bureaucracy (and vice versa). Most decisions are influenced to some extent by large numbers of people. Even where control may seem to be concentrated, it is usually *balanced* by the power of others in other spheres: that of captains of industry by trade unions, consumer groups, and other commercial organisations; that of political leaders by opposition parties, the press, industry, unions and public opinion generally; that of union leaders by employers, governments (and other union leaders); and so on. Frequently there is a struggle within each group as well as between them. 'Elites' themselves compete with each other. Thus the concept of a single, composite 'power-elite', a ruling class, conspiring together to control the masses, such as is sometimes suggested, bears no relation to reality (unless it means that there are usually fewer people at the top of each organisation than at the bottom, not a very profound discovery). The real position is always that of a *balance* of influences: men are influencing and being influenced at the same time.

But influence is not evenly distributed. Nor is it rationally distributed. There are huge variations in the opportunities and effectiveness of different kinds of influence.

In considering the distribution of influence, there are two points above all to consider. First why do some influences have more weight than others? Secondly, what weight *should* be attached to each?

First, which influences now count for most? What normally occurs is not a simple battle among groups, each representing

certain sections of the population. Most people belong to many
different groups, each engaging in different types of activity and
influence at once. Each group is itself subject to many influences
that surround them all the time. Influence takes place both
laterally (from one group to another) and vertically (from public to
authorities and vice versa). Nevertheless some groups clearly
possess more influence than others. Differences depend both on the
differential *opportunities* for influence and on the differential
effectiveness of each influence. Both will vary greatly, between
individuals and groups, and from one type of decision to another.

The difference in opportunity for influence is perhaps the most
important single factor determining how far a system is 'democratic'. In other words whether influence counts one for one is
much more significant than whether votes count one for one.

One important factor affecting this is the difference in the *timing*
of different influences. Groups that can bring their influence to
bear at a very early stage (for example while legislation is still being
prepared) are more likely to make it effective than those which
exert it later (e.g. only while a bill is already being debated in
parliament, when it is often too late for any major change). It is
where legislation is *prepared*, not where it is passed, that the major
decisions are made. Even the cabinet very often only confirms a
decision that is largely taken elsewhere: in the department
concerned, in cabinet committees, or by the minister concerned
and the Prime Minister between them.[9] Knowledge of exactly *who*
it is important to contact and influence when is another factor that
will have an important impact on the effectiveness of different
influences in a large-scale political structure.

Secondly, the amount of influence exerted depends on who it is
shared with. Significant influence today is nearly always collective,
not individual. Outside the decision-makers themselves (and even
they, as we saw, are limited and controlled by others), only a very
few - a respected elder statesman, a retired civil servant or an
eminent bishop - still have (as did many in earlier times) an
individual authority. Normally the lone voice will be discounted
precisely because it is a lone voice. The secretary general of the
mineworkers' union is listened to because he is secretary general,
not because of his personal qualities. Even the minister is often
heard because he speaks with the authority of his department, not
because he personally is thought to have wise and profound things
to say. Because decision-making is increasingly institutionalised,

there is less scope for any individual, alone and by himself, to exert a large influence over it.

The influences that are effective are those that are *organised*. Influence thus depends not only on collective will, but on collective skill in organisation and presentation. As we saw in Chapter 1, individuals today have mainly collective interests, as members of a particular industry, occupation or locality. They are thus often organised to promote these interests with governments on that basis: through their employers' association, through their unions, through a local authority or a residents' association. Influences are respected mainly *because* they are representative of those interests. Even the procedures of influence in modern societies become institutionalised: in the recognition of representative interest-groups, in the appointment of their members to particular committees, in the invitation of a delegation from it to see a minister.

If influence is to be justly distributed, one essential is to know how far the bodies that exert recognised influence are truly representative of those whose interests are concerned. Partici-pation in pressure-groups is often at present restricted to a fairly small number, with little machinery for assuring that they are representative. This applies even to the broadest organisations through which influence is exerted. Political parties, for example, may express the demands of their activists, their MPs or their leaders, rather than those of their members generally, let alone of their electors. Newspapers and television stations may represent the views of their editors, or owners, or commentators, rather than of their readers or viewers generally. Pressure-groups may promote the interests of their leaders or most powerful members, rather than of their membership as a whole.

In each case the formulation of policy is restricted to a small group who may not be fully representative, even of the interests concerned, let alone of the public generally. Only those who draw up the election manifesto of a political party, who decide the line of action of the BMA or the TGWU, or who determine the editorial policy of a newspaper, are able to decide what type of *demand* shall be put forward at any one time; it is they, in other words, who determine the crucial inputs into the political system. In many cases the degree of influence they have will depend to a large extent not on any accurate assessment of how representative they are, or how genuine is the case presented, but on how vocal are the interests involved. And the resources available to different groups for publicising their views, the publicity accorded to them, their access to departments or ministers, may bear no relation to the extent that they reflect widely-held views.

This leads to the second question we posed: how much influence *should* be exerted by different individuals or groups on each type of decision? What degree of influence is *appropriate* to the person's capacities or knowledge or position; or *excessive*, in relation to the type of problem confronted and the other people affected? On general questions of policy is it more democratic for governments to pay most attention to the views of members of parliament, who represent the electorate and have no special interest but may not be experts on the subject concerned; to a party conference, representing the political grass-roots but not representing electors and still more inexpert; to bureaucrats, who *are* experts but wholly without responsibility; to the views expressed by the press, which claims to represent public opinion, but may not; to the various interest-groups concerned, who are closely affected, but also strongly partial; or to the views of the majority, as expressed in opinion polls, undoubtedly representative but lacking in expertise and knowledge of the facts? Does the fact that the press builds up a campaign against a particular policy mean that to act democratically the government should 'heed popular views' and give way; or should it 'stand firm' in resisting? Or should governments (as normally at present) *pretend* to listen to the views generally expressed, but in fact take account only of the technical advice of their experts?

There are a few propositions that would be fairly generally accepted. First, a government should promote widespread public discussion *before* any commitment in principle is reached (at present if a proposal is accepted by a party caucus and placed in a manifesto, it is only the *means* which are thereafter open to discussion). Secondly, if influence on decisions is to be equal, everybody, press and party, public and pressure-groups, must not only have equal *rights*, but so far as possible equal *opportunities*, to make their views known and their views felt. Thirdly, it follows that any position of *special* influence, in access to ministries, to the press and broadcasting media, to the political parties or parliament, should be eliminated. Fourthly, the views and influence of those who have a special and direct interest in the subject concerned should be particularly carefully sought and listened to, but not necessarily especially obeyed (this must of course include *all* those affected, consumers as well as producers, workers as well as industrialists, common-sensible men as well as cranks). Fifthly, such influences and representations should be made known publicly, so that all suspicions of special or secret influence are dispelled. Sixth, the final decision should be taken by a body in which all interested parties are represented directly or indirectly, and not by some authority with a special interest, say a ministry of agriculture, tied to a single interest-group. Finally, governments and other authorities should explain all decisions in full, and the reasons that have led to them, before they are implemented, and be ready to think again: in this way the degree of influence that special groups or interests may have may be checked, and, if necessary, counteracted before irreversible action is taken.

Some problems are more difficult. In discussing decisions concerning a school, for example, how much weight should be attached to the opinions of the headmaster, of the staff as a whole, of the parents, of the pupils, of the school governors, of the local authority, of the Ministry of Education or of local residents? How much influence over the distribution of national investment should be exercised by central government, by local planning boards, by local authorities, the CBI, the TUC, each individual industry and each individual firm? In reaching such a judgement considerations of 'fair' representation need to be balanced against considerations relating to the efficiency of decision-making in terms of speed and results. Assessments of this kind have hardly begun to be made by political scientists. The exact amount of influence to be exerted by different individuals and groups on different kinds of decisions will always be to some extent a matter of judgement. But at least the attempt needs to be made.

In considering all these questions the most crucial point concerns the factor we considered in Chapter 1: the balance between the *upward-moving* influences from society to government, and the *downward-moving* influences the other way. For while many groups and individuals are seeking at all times to influence governments in the decisions they reach, the government will itself be influencing, more or less deliberately, the society as a whole. In extreme form this is seen in a totalitarian system where all communications media are in the hands of the government, which uses them to influence the population in favour of its own policies, and which can indeed manufacture opinion. In the Soviet Union today, for example, almost every effective influence is downward-moving, so reducing the likelihood that policies will reflect spontaneous popular wishes. In some societies messages may be mainly downwards below a certain level in society (from feudal lords to peasants, from bureaucrats to people), mainly upwards (from feudal lords to king, from bureaucrats to minister) above that level. Where the downward-moving messages from government are very powerful and very numerous, those moving upward, from parliament, press, pressure groups and public as a whole, are consequently weakened and ineffective.

One of the major trends of the modern world is that downwards movements are strong in all societies. The purposes of the state tend increasingly to dictate the choices available to the citizen. In any advanced society the need for coordination, planning, supervision, the complexity and technicality of many decisions, encourage the downward-moving forces; while the secrecy of much decision-making discourages upward-moving ones. Even if the government does not consciously undertake 'news management', influence the supply of news on particular topics to justify its own policies, it will have public relations officers, and press departments for particular ministries, to give information, and will employ perpetual public comment by ministers to explain and justify policies to the country. The upward-moving influences on the other hand are discouraged and depreciated – dismissed as inexpert, prejudiced or ignorant: so it is 'statesmanlike' to ignore them.

How far, therefore, the system is 'democratic', is really responsive to the desires of individuals and the demands of groups, will depend not only on the balance of influences in general; but, above all else, on the balance between the upward and downward-moving messages in society as a whole. How far are the citizens able to exercise effective influence on the state; how far, on the contrary, is it they who increasingly come under the influence that the state exerts on them?

6.4 *The Diffusion of Influence*

In socialist and non-socialist states alike, therefore, there exist, in a world of large-scale organisation, many factors which prevent the ordinary citizen from feeling he enjoys any genuine share in

controlling, or even in significantly influencing, the decisions
reached in his society.

How could the citizen be given a more meaningful and more
equal influence than he has today? We have seen how little he
acquires through the system of parliamentary elections. He
possesses, it is true, the right of expelling a government which has
manifestly failed. But this gives him no opportunity to pronounce
on individual policies. To vote one lot out, he has to vote in
another, complete with an appendage of policies of which he may
totally disapprove. He must vote each time for a *package* of
proposals which cannot be unwrapped. Even on matters outside
the party system – the so-called private members' issues, such as
abortion, divorce, or capital punishment – the elector has no
influence: for here the MP will follow his own conscience rather
than that of his electors. However assiduously or passionately the
citizen may write to his MP demanding his support for a certain
viewpoint, therefore, this is largely ineffectual since on most such
matters the MP's mind is made up – either by his party leaders or
by himself.

How then can influence be more *genuinely* diffused? There are
several small changes which would make the present system
somewhat more responsive to popular wishes. If citizens would join
political parties in much larger numbers than they do now, those
parties, in framing their policies, would more closely reflect the
aspirations of the mass of the populations. Decision-making *within*
the parties should be democratised, so that the choice of election
programmes – by far the most important decision made within the
whole of the nation's life – the selection of candidates, the recall of
MP's and other matters, would be influenced by the great mass of
the membership, instead of by the small groups who now
determine these questions. In parliament, a far larger number of
decisions could be left to the free vote of MPs; for while it is
reasonable, and in some ways helpful to the voter, that the MP he
elects is committed to the general *principles* of particular policies
laid down in a manifesto, there is no reason why backbenchers
should not be allowed much greater discretion in deciding the ways
the policies are *implemented* (for example, at the committee stage of
bills), as well as in deciding other matters not mentioned in the
manifesto at all. Finally, to assist the legislature in relation to the
all-powerful executive, new, more powerful parliamentary committees, able to demand information, explanations and justi-

fications from ministers, and other procedures of a similar kind, should be established: only this could make parliamentary pressure a more effective influence on the executive than it is today.

None of this, however, would overcome the main difficulty we have mentioned: that the citizen at present has no influence over the decisions on *particular* policies. Here the obvious way of overcoming the difficulty is through the regular use of referenda. For this is the only way in which the elector can be given the chance to have a say about specific questions. Many of the arguments traditionally used against referenda have little substance. It is said that they derogate from the 'sovereignty of parliament'; but most parliaments handed over effective sovereignty to the executive decades ago – the referendum would be on the contrary a way of bringing sovereignty *back* from the executive to the people as a whole. It is said that the issues are too complicated for the people to judge; but this is a highly arrogant, even aristocratic argument, precisely comparable to those used against universal suffrage a century or so ago, and invariably made by those who consider they know better than the 'people' what is good for their welfare. It is said that most of the problems of government are far too complex and detailed for ordinary people to be in a position to make a rational judgement about; but in fact they would be asked only to decide questions of general principle – should abortion be permitted, should censorship be tightened or relaxed, should public houses stay open later at night, should we drive on the right-hand side of the road instead of the left, should Scotland be independent from Britain? – and so on, matters which (like the question whether Britain should join the EEC) the lowliest person in Britain has as much right to judge as the cleverest expert in the land; and a particular referendum could, if required, be made consultative only. Again, it is held that the results of referenda are highly conservative; but this depends on the amount and style of leadership given during the campaign, and there is no more reason for conservative results in referenda than in elections (it is mainly the referenda in highly conservative areas, such as Switzerland, and certain states in the US, which have led to this judgement). Or it is suggested that there would never be agreement on the questions to be put, and the way they should be worded; but this is a problem that has been overcome in those countries and states where referenda are common, and could as easily be overcome here.[10] And so on. There is no limit to the

number of arguments that can be put against the system by those
who are already hostile. They are at root all elitist arguments,
based on the complacent conviction that most people cannot be
trusted to decide the matters that will closely affect their lives, but
should have these decisions taken for them by others who know
best.

There could also be *local* referenda on matters affecting particular areas: for example, systems of education, transport, planning
questions, housing policy and such matters within the area.
Indeed, the more decisions can be localised, the more effective is
the consultation. Only where the locality is relatively small would
the citizen be given the feeling he enjoyed a significant share in the
decision made. A 500th or even a 5000th share in a decision is
worth far more than a 50 millionth.

Another way of diffusing influence would be by a conscious
attempt to *promote* the establishment of groups to represent
particular interests and viewpoints. The emergence of pressure-
groups need not be the sinister threat to broadly-based government
which is sometimes suggested. Such groups, provided they are
genuinely representative, can be the instrument for expressing and
representing the views of ordinary people in a much more direct
way than any other. For they possess one asset which other forms of
influence do not: they are highly specific in their demands. The
citizen who joins such a group (unlike the one who joins a political
party) knows that its influence and activity will be devoted entirely
and specifically to a particular objective: preventing cruelty to
animals, helping the homeless or the one-parent family, protecting
the environment, looking after the interests of motorists or pedes-
trians, or whatever it may be.

If influence is to be better distributed, the logical course,
therefore, is not to decry or restrict the activities of pressure-groups,
but to seek to *develop*, and to balance, their influence. For they
could in fact be one of the most significant ways of providing the
individual citizen with more effective and discriminating influence
over the way he is governed. They are far more sharply focused in
activity than parliament, the media, and the other main channels
of influence. They are accessible, as those are not, in the sense that
anybody can join as many or as few of them as he wishes. They can
be formed more easily – and once formed may be readily influenced
to adopt a new viewpoint or policy, as a party or an organ of the
press cannot.

But at present such groups differ widely in influence according to factors unrelated to the volume of opinion they represent; according to their resources; their efficiency and organisational capacity; their leadership; their contacts with the government departments concerned; and so on. Again, some groups and causes have no organisation at all to represent them. Although sometimes the existence of a pressure-group may be said to reflect the extent of feelings on a particular subject, the reverse is not the case. The educated and the middle class are more articulate and active than others in such activities. The chance that there once existed an angry and dynamic individual who was concerned on a particular issue, while for another cause there was not, may be the decisive factor. Again certain groups (the TUC and the CBI in Britain, for example) enjoy an automatic status of great importance, while other groups representing equally large numbers (say the house-wives or the old) may be ignored: a ministry of agriculture may automatically consult farmers in negotiating farm prices but consumers not at all. A small number of people who feel strongly *against* a certain case or proposal (say vivisection, noise, or football on the Sabbath) are more likely to have an organisation, and to campaign vigorously, than a large number who feel less strongly in *favour*. Finally the whole system functions at present often in far too secret and hole-in-corner a manner, so no one can know what influence is being exerted on whom by what groups.

To equalise their influence such groups should be provided with more *recognised* channels for contacts: recognised times and opportunities for the lobbying of Ministers, MPs and civil servants;[11] better facilities, on broadcasting and TV channels and in the newspapers, for presenting their case to the general public, and on an equal basis; possibly offices in or close to the Houses of Parliament. Government departments would be obliged to maintain close and continuing contacts with such groups. MPs might publicly act as their spokesmen in parliament. The widest possible membership of such groups would be encouraged. The media would be encouraged to provide time and space for their views. Equalising the techniques and *opportunities* of contact in that way would reduce the differences in influence among them that now exist.

But, as we have seen, by far the most important reason for the difficulty the citizen has in exercising effective influence on the way he is governed is simply the scale of the modern state and the remoteness of administration. Authority and powers have been progressively transferred to higher levels so that all the important decisions increasingly are taken at levels that appear infinitely distant to the ordinary citizen. Power is more and more centralised, thus more and more exerted at the point where the individual has least weight. At the same time government is not only more remote but more technical, and the decisions to be taken depend increasingly on quantities of detailed knowledge and statistical material which is far beyond the comprehension of the average citizen (and usually of the average member of parliament too)

If therefore the citizen is to be given a greater sense of control over his destiny, there is a more fundamental change required. This is the transfer of authority *downwards* to lower levels; the breaking-down of existing units of authority into far smaller units. There is a clear logical reason for this: as the size of the majority increases, the less valuable a share in it becomes. The remoteness of national governments, and even of regional and county authorities, makes any true sense of control by the citizen over their activities, any genuinely felt identification with their purposes, however representative they may be in theory, to all intents impossible. The main essence of democracy, the sense of consent in decisions reached, is lacking. Equally important, a true diversity among different communities becomes impossible where all are submerged in the vast consensus of a single all-embracing national power.

Yet today, though the nation is far too large to provide any genuine sentiment of self-government for its members, it adds to its power all the time. Conversely, the real living units, the village, the small town, and the local community within a town, are increasingly *deprived* of their powers, and merged within larger, amorphous administrative areas, on grounds of 'functional efficiency'. Non-political units, the club and association, alone remain small enough for a genuine sense of identification and active participation, yet these are altogether without powers.

There must always remain a few decisions that can only be taken at a relatively high level. There will always be need at least of *coordination* in certain fields. But this should be so far as possible voluntary, not imposed. Today many tasks are performed by large-scale organisations that could be performed, with only marginally less efficiency, and with infinitely greater satisfaction for those participating, in much smaller units. The basic principle should be that every group would itself make the decisions that affect them most closely. School policy would be decided primarily by parents and teachers; local authorities would exert a small amount of influence, and national authorities none. Local planning decisions would be made mainly by the parish, or even the street, only the broad outlines by the county. Social services would be community-linked, not vast, sprawling administrative monstrosities, with more administrators than social workers. Local institutions would be restored, to run the affairs of genuine, living communities, each of only two or three hundred people. Even within cities, small communities, corresponding to parishes in the countryside and the focus for local loyalties, [12] might be the agents of local action. In the country, villages would run their own affairs. Districts would take over powers now undertaken by counties, and regions many powers now undertaken by the state, both administrative and economic.

There might be economies of scale that would be sacrificed under such a system. But it may be more important sometimes to lose money for the sake of social satisfaction, than to save it for economic efficiency. The initial presumption always would be in favour of local independence rather than central direction: only where communities voluntarily *chose* to work together would this take place. But the community itself would be the basic unit.

One way of encouraging diversity, as well as of encouraging a greater sense of local identity, would be by a greater use than at present of the principle of indirect representation. If parishes were represented in cities, and cities in counties or other regional authorities, and all of these at the national level, perhaps in the second chamber, each unit would retain a greater significance within the minds of the public; electors would have representatives who seemed primarily of their locality, rather than of their party. Such a system might too reduce some of the clashes of authority that so often take place between authorities at different levels. And it should certainly reduce the sense of remoteness that direct representation alone now brings about.

To bring any true sense of independence and initiative, local authorities would need to be given financial autonomy: the power to undertake as much or as little expenditure as they choose without special legislation (in Britain at present a local authority cannot spend a penny without statutory authority and may have to have a by-law passed through parliament to start a laundry). This would enable each community to establish its own style and way of life. Some would establish many municipal activities and undertakings,

while others would leave everything to private initiative. Some
might seek to establish a highly egalitarian community, while
others would stress diversity; some would seek a great deal of
communal social activity, while others would leave its members
the maximum of privacy and independence; some would establish
an authoritarian, others a libertarian community. Local communities, rather than nations, might then determine the character
of society for their members; and so make it possible once more
that diversity in social style that today is being everywhere lost.
And because authority was at last closer, some of the original
ideals of democratic theory – the provision for the citizen of a
sense of control over his own destiny – might begin to be restored.

But it is not only within states that influence is unevenly
distributed today, but between them too. One effect of the
domination of the state everywhere is that inequalities, as we saw,
become collective rather than personal. While some of the grosser
inequalities between individuals have been reduced through the
machinery established by the state, those between states, and
between individuals in different states, are unaffected: indeed
inequalities of the latter kind, far from being reduced, become
greater all the time. The inequalities in wealth are reflected in
inequalities in influence. Here, too, the institutions of the state
serve rather to uphold and maintain existing inequalities, rather
than to reduce them. Only more effective world institutions, in
which influence was distributed according to population rather
than economic power, could serve to establish a fairer distribution
of influence at the world level. Thus it is not only downwards, to
more local authorities, that the nation-state may need to shed some
of its authority, but also upwards to the world level; to the
embryonic international institutions already existing, or those
more effective ones which may replace them (see Chapter 10
below).

If socialism is concerned with a more equal distribution of
influence, as well as of property rights, it thus clearly requires some
broader objective than state socialism, whose effect is only to
promote the power of individual states. Only a radical restructur-
ing of institutions *within* states would provide the ordinary citizen
with a greater sense that he is able to influence the decisions that
dominate his life. Only a strengthening of institutions *among* states
will equalise influence between them. Only a shedding of the

inflated powers of the state, both downwards to the small community, and upwards to the world level, will achieve the ideal of a more equal sharing of power and responsibility which has always been one of the most deeply held aspirations of socialism.

7 Inequality in Economic Power

7.1 *The Concentration of Economic Power*

But it is not only a more equal distribution of political influence that socialists have demanded. They have been even more concerned to secure greater equality in economic power.

For the early socialists one of the prime defects of the capitalist system was the concentration of economic power in the hands of the few, the privileged, the owners or enterprisers: in a word of 'capital'. This made the worker into a wholly dependent creature, a tool used by the capitalist for his own profit.

For Marx and many early socialists, this concentration of economic power, and the inequality that resulted, derived from the private *ownership* of the means of production. This concept of the ownership of 'capital', in Marx's writing, is a somewhat simple one. Marx tended to see the owner as a single figure who could use his power as proprietor to dominate and control the lives of those who worked for him.

Often (as in the famous conversation illustrating surplus product in Chapter 7 of Book I of *Capital*) the concept of 'capital' is represented by a single capitalist, the supplier of capital, the owner and employer (though not the manager), all in one. Marx may have intended this as symbolic only, but it is illustrative of his essentially abstract and non-empirical approach to the capitalist system, even as it then existed. For a fundamental change in that system was taking place during his lifetime: the establishment of the limited liability company. The absentee shareholder, never attending company meetings but drawing his dividend and his capital gains, today the dominant, perhaps archetypal, figure within the system, was already born: a figure who had *ownership* but no meaningful *control*. Yet this figure is scarcely considered by Marx, or by most other nineteenth-century socialist writers. They think characteristically of the 'capitalist', the 'entrepreneur' or the 'employer', in abstract terms, as against the 'worker' (who is also not characterised, for example, as skilled or unskilled, white-collar or clerical).

Even in Marx's day, there were a number of varied types of financial structure which he scarcely analysed. But the situation today is still more complex. With the development of many kinds of intermediary between the individual shareholder and the company itself, the development of the institutional investor, of complex interrelationships between different companies and holding companies, the concept of 'capital' becomes more hazy. The vast majority of ordinary shares of companies today are owned by bodies such as insurance companies, investment trusts, pensions funds, unit trusts, banks and others. In some capitalist countries, especially Japan and West Germany, most of the finance of industry comes from banks rather than from individual investors. In developing countries many private businesses are financed by state 'development banks' or other publicly-owned institutions. Through these intermediaries, ownership becomes still further divorced from control; and still more remote from those who actually work within the enterprises.

In these circumstances it becomes harder to define exactly where ultimate responsibility lies. Is the 'capitalist' the shareholder who subscribed to the company in the first place and later sold his shares; the shareholder who buys them subsequently but has never provided any capital to the company; the insurance policy-holder who merely pays a premium to the insurance company; that company itself which invests in ordinary shares; the pension fund which purchases shares; the pensioner who benefits from the distribution of that fund; the bank which lends funds for expansion, but retains no permanent holding; the debenture-holder who has first claim on the profits but receives only fixed interest; or the non-voting shareholder who has invested in the company but has no control? Is the full-time managing director who owns a few shares and makes the key decisions a capitalist? Or is he a hired employee engaged by capital?

The fact is that capital itself has now become collective. Institutions rather than individuals occupy the dominant place within it. And in the process they become even more remote from those actually engaged.

At the same time, management, while now largely divorced from ownership, also becomes more remote from workers. With the increase in scale of operation management grows many times in numbers and power. It takes over effective control of the company from the shareholders who are still its nominal owners. Under these circumstances, the vital decisions of capitalism are taken by the manager, not the 'capitalist'. And it is the manager who in the immediate sense exercises domination over the worker. It is he with whom the worker comes into contact, of whom he is conscious, against whom resentments and antagonisms develop, rather than the shareholder with whom he had no dealings and of whom he is scarcely aware.

Marx believed that the domination of the worker, his subjection to external forces, resulted from the system of ownership. Under socialism, with the abolition of private property, it would automatically be ended. The change in ownership would transform productive relations.

But in socialist states in fact the change in *ownership* has not affected the system of *control*. The same type of management bureaucracy appears here too. Though capital is dead, the enterprises, the corporation, the organisation and its management, vast, impersonal, disembodied, yet far more powerful in its impact on men's lives than any individual capitalist could be in Marx's day, still remain only too alive.

As a result, the worker in the socialist state, or in the nationalised enterprise in Western states, is as much as any elsewhere the victim of 'alienation'. Marx's description of this condition (derived from the ideas of Feuerbach on alienation in religion) is as follows:

> In what does the alienation of labour consist? First, that the work is *external* to the worker, that it is not a part of his nature, that consequently he does not fulfil himself in his work but denies himself, has a feeling of misery, not of well-being, does not develop freely a physical and mental energy, but is physically exhausted and mentally debased. The worker therefore feels himself at home only during his leisure, whereas at work he feels homeless. His work is not voluntary but imposed, *forced labour*. It is not the satisfaction of a need, but only a *means* for satisfying other needs. Its alien character is clearly shown by the fact that as soon as there is no physical or other compulsion it is evaded like the plague. Finally, the alienated character of work for the worker appears in the fact that it is not his work, but work for someone else, that in work he does not belong to himself but to another person.[1]

Much of this is an excellent account of the position of many industrial workers today. But the description could be applied without distinction to work in a nationalised industry or in a private one; and to work in a socialist state as in a capitalist one. In either case, work is external, a means for satisfying other needs, work for someone else or something else, rather than for the worker himself.

For the real cause of his situation is not, as Marx suggested, the system of ownership. It is its scale, and the forms of *control* that result. It is the vast, impersonal and apparently inhuman character of the industrial machine, of the business enterprise, of the modern productive process, that above all induces the sense of alienation, mechanisation and dehumanisation. Because the technology and the scale are no different in a socialist state from a capitalist state, in a nationalised corporation from a private one, the prevalent attitude of the worker towards his work and his place within it is also much the same; and indeed is not essentially different from that described in the above passage from Marx.

What might influence a significant change in his attitude towards his work is not, therefore, a change in the system of ownership (however necessary this might be for other reasons, for example, to reduce inequalities in property or income) but a change in the system of control. Yet under state socialism the concentration of control is not less than under capitalism but greater. For while under capitalism ownership and control have become divorced, under state socialism they are once again united. And while under capitalism control remains still to some extent divided, among the boards and managements of many different companies, under state socialism it is even more concentrated: in the hands of the all-powerful state itself, which controls every industry and every enterprise alike.

7.2 *Collective Saving and Collective Investment*

Thus the concentration of economic power in the hands of the few, and the dependence of the great mass of the workers on these few, which was the main source of concern among early socialist writers, is not significantly different today, and is as great under state socialism as it was under capitalism. It is indeed if anything greater.

But there is another sense in which modern socialist states largely reproduce the conditions of capitalist states.

In both cases, as we saw earlier (p. 20), saving and investment have today largely become collective. The process of 'accumulation', which Marx and many others once saw as the basic source of inequalities among individuals, is now largely undertaken by collectivities, and is equally the source of inequalities among them. The greater part of saving in the modern world is done by industrial companies; by state corporations; and by governments. The internal savings of companies are far more important today than personal savings as a source of investment funds; and increasingly in socialist states the internal savings of state corporations become an important factor there too. Governments equally save huge sums through their tax revenues, besides borrowing more from elsewhere. Even the external sources of funds today are also collective; banks, insurance companies, investment trusts and other institutions, rather than private individuals as before. It is these institutions rather than the private shareholder or 'capitalist' who provide these funds, and who can now decide to what uses savings are put.

Secondly, as a result, investment as well as saving becomes collective, rather than personal; and this too is true in capitalist and socialist economies alike. The same collectivities which save funds decide how and where to invest them, usually in large-scale projects. One effect is that investment is today increasingly coordinated rather than competitive. Among private companies there is collaboration, tacit or explicit, to share the market. In state-controlled economies the entire system is based on coordination. In both cases it results largely from the increase in scale. Where a new steel mill will meet, say, a fifth of the total market – or even a tenth or a twentieth – it becomes essential that it is not built twice: there must be some element of planning, or at least mutual knowledge of intentions, if investment resources are not to be catastrophically wasted. Coordination is particularly vital in certain fields: the establishment of communications facilities, the development of fuel and power resources, the location of industry. But it becomes necessary in nearly all large industries with high capital investment. Thus, in the West as much as in the East, increasing centralisation and coordination of large-scale decisions, especially investment decisions, comes about.

Thirdly, much of this collective investment, in capitalist and socialist economies alike, is by governments. Governments have control over expenditure in transport, health, social services, state industries, regional aids and other government spending. They subsidise, or invest directly in, particular industries or firms. They give tax relief for investment and for depreciation, sometimes with special favours for particular industries or areas. They decide what should be spent in technical education, in expanding industrial training and retraining, in export promotion and commercial work overseas and for what industries. Above all governments provide planning machinery for the direct and deliberate coordination of investment decisions: to determine priorities and to avoid over-lapping (and therefore risk). Thus it is now no longer the 'investor', nor even the manager or director, who makes the major decisions to allocate funds. It is the government itself.

Fourthly, one effect of the fact that saving and investment are collective is that investment usually stays put. It is normally more attractive for a company or state enterprise to concentrate on the markets they know, and to use surplus funds for expansion in the field in which it has the greatest experience, techniques and resources. Investment therefore tends to remain concentrated where the markets are largest (that is in the states already richest); and to stay in the fields that have produced the largest profits in the past, rather than moving to those that may prove most profitable in the future. Among governments, which now undertake a large part of investment, this is even more the case. Their collective investment is overwhelmingly in their own state. Thus the investment funds of one nation are overwhelmingly reinvested in the same nation. For this reason too, investment stays put.

Fifthly, the collectivisation of saving and investment affects relative rewards as well. Internal savings are an increasingly large source of investment funds. This means that rewards paid to shareholders may be the return not only for their own contri-bution of funds, but for the internally saved capital as well. This is justified on the argument that the funds internally saved them-selves 'belonged' to the shareholders. But it has never been shown why the rewards for increasing efficiency and increasing success should go to those who have contributed least to achieving it, the passive shareholders, rather than to those – the management, staff and workers – who might reasonably claim to have done something by their own efforts to win them. This appropriation of profits was classically justified by the 'risks' the provider of capital undertook.

But in practice, as we have just seen, the collective character of investment means that this risk has now virtually disappeared. While there is some variation in the rate of profits and dividends, they rarely fail altogether, for coordination was precisely to prevent this.

The new scale of operation also affects the sacrifice or 'abstinence', which saving is said to require. The mammoth corporation, with huge turnover in a number of different fields, and only limited competition, can undertake collective saving and investment, with little effort or inconvenience (internal saving is often higher among very big firms than in others). Governments in wealthy countries can undertake very high rates of saving with no great effort for themselves or for their populations. In both cases (as has always been the case among individuals), the degree of sacrifice saving represents is determined by the level of wealth *previously* acquired. The investment that is possible may thus vary, not so much according to the relative success or prospects of the firm concerned, but according to the amount of internal saving which is possible for it. Volumes of savings and investment that are extremely difficult or impossible for a poor economy or a small enterprise are easy for a rich one. Volumes of saving and investment, and therefore rewards, that involve no effort at all for a rich country or a large firm are out of the question for a poor one.

Today therefore both saving and investment are transformed: are collective rather than individual. There are a few occupations in which the individual himself still makes the decisions to spend on new productive resources: the farmer, the doctor, the tradesman and the very small businessman may invest in this way. But even here, the money required normally must be raised from a bank or a finance company whose judgement will therefore often be the decisive one. By far the greater number of investment decisions are made, however, by collective bodies, large corporations, government departments, nationalised undertakings, and other organisations which, with the growth in scale of operation, control an increasing proportion of the production and distribution of resources in every advanced country. These decisions will be made institutionally: by a group of people (say a board of directors), perhaps on the recommendation of another group (say the managing director and his staff), and perhaps confirmed by some other group (a bank, a merchant bank, the house of issue, or underwriters).

One effect of this is that to a large extent the whim, or inspiration or daring speculation, of a single bold capitalist or entrepreneur, risking his own money at his own discretion, is today largely eliminated. So also, because the consequences can be better calculated, is much of the risk. Investment in a single project today, say a steel mill or a new automobile plant, or an electronics factory, may be in tens or hundreds of millions of dollars, and since huge sums of money are involved, it is inevitably necessary to be very sure the investment will pay off. More careful calculation must be undertaken than in the past of the likely market for the product, of the probable costs, of the capacity already existing elsewhere, of likely trends within the economy as a whole, and many other factors, before the investment is undertaken in the first place. While in Marx's day a risky venture that failed, though it could be expensive for the individual enterprise concerned, might represent for the economy as a whole a worthwhile price for progress, today the failure of any major project may represent a huge cost, not only for the enterprise and for its workpeople, but for the economy as a whole. Investment has necessarily become increasingly deliberate, calculated and rational. But the system for allocating its reward has not been correspondingly transformed.

7.3 *The distribution of economic power*

Thus in both non-socialist and socialist states, the ownership and control of economic resources have become still more concentrated. Saving and investment have been collectivised – are made by a small elite group on behalf of the collectivity as a whole. The power of the ordinary worker, or the ordinary citizen, over economic decisions is less than ever, since the scale or organisation is bigger. The sense of alienation for the worker, the feeling of being without control of his own destiny, is even worse than before, for the same reason. The *working* satisfaction made available to the worker, the quality of life he obtains in his work, once the supreme aim of socialism, has thus become less than ever, whether he works within a collectivised capitalism, or within state socialism.

Classical socialism, as we saw, conceived that, when the productive instruments of the country were taken into public ownership, the way of life of the worker would be automatically transformed. Usually it was ownership and control of the economy *as a whole* that was demanded by such writers. It was the state's acquisition of productive resources which would bring about the change.

But this was a logical fallacy. To influence the quality of life, and sense of control, of the worker, it was shared ownership and control *within the enterprise* that might have been expected to have some impact. But this idea was not entertained by most socialist writers. Equally the almost exclusive concern of Marx and others in his day was with *ownership* – far less relevant to the worker's sense of dependence or alienation than its control.

The distinction between ownership and control was scarcely thought of by early socialist writers. Marx said little about the control of industry in a socialist state; still less about control of an individual enterprise. It is possible to look through all his works and find virtually no recognition that such a problem even existed, let alone how it should be solved. In listing the measures to be taken after the socialist revolution, the Communist Manifesto mentions

> . . . centralisation of credit in the hands of the State, by means of a national bank with state capital and an exclusive monopoly . . . centralisation of the means of communication and transport in the hands of the State; extension of factories and instruments of production owned by the State.

But neither here nor elsewhere is there any detailed consideration of the way these productive resources should be managed in a socialist state: neither the means for the general planning of the economy, nor for the management of individual enterprises. It is merely taken for granted that, since the ownership of industry and its enterprises would be taken into 'the hands of the state', so would its control. And once that was achieved and the state itself controlled by all the workers, all difficult and perplexing problems would be abolished.

The belief of socialist theorists that once property was abolished, and all production resources taken into the control of the state, all conflict and difficulties would be removed implied that not only would the interests of the state and the interests of the workers as a whole coincide: the interests of the state and that of the workers in any particular *industry* would also coincide. Nor was this all. The interests of the workers in a particular *enterprise* and that of the state would also be identical. And the interests of workers in different industries and enterprises should never be in conflict. The workers would own, and control and manage, and all problems would be solved. It was on this assumption of identity of interest of workers in different industries, and of both with the interests and decisions of the state, that the economic systems in the Soviet Union and East European countries were first set up.

But it may be doubted how far workers and citizens in such societies do always identify with the state that controls their work. Even within the enterprise management is remote and unresponsive. The average worker may rarely even see the managing director of the factory in which he works. But if the manager of an enterprise appears remote, how much more do the controllers in a distant state ministry, directing the affairs of an industry, or the board of a huge nationalised corporation, employing hundreds of thousands or millions of men, scattered around many different enterprises?

It is to deal with this problem of the remoteness of management that there have been attempts, both in the West and in one or two socialist states, to establish forms of 'industrial democracy': ways in which the worker may be given a sense of control over the decisions ruling his life. Clearly no system of workers' control can do away with the need for management and managers. There must always remain certain individuals whose function is to reach certain types of decision, to initiate certain types of communication, to give certain types of instruction. There has not yet been, and probably never will be, a system in which all the workers make every decision in the factory by a majority vote. In one or two cases, as we shall see, a workers' council may appoint, or elect, or at least have power to dismiss, a manager; but there always remain certain spheres subject to management decision inside the factory. The important question, therefore, is, the degree of *influence* over management which may be exerted by workers or their representatives, in which fields this shall operate, and how it shall be exercised.

In West Germany, under legislation first passed in 1951 but amplified more than once since, at least one-third of the members of the supervisory board in every German company must be representatives of the employees, elected by secret ballot. Secondly, one member of the management board, the labour director, is himself appointed by this supervisory board, and must have the support of a majority of the workers' representatives on that board. In addition there is a works council, elected by all employees over eighteen by secret ballot every two years. This council concludes all agreements on wages, piece-rates and wage systems (where there is no wider collective agreement), working conditions, work rules, timing of holidays, training and some other matters. It must be consulted over all proposals involving redundancies or new engagements, mergers, the transfer of departments and major changes in production. It deals with complaints and grievances. And it administers the social welfare facilities within the plant. This works council however, which performs functions not very different from those undertaken by union representatives or shop stewards' committees in Britain, is of far less importance in management than the supervisory board, and still less than the management board itself. Within the supervisory board the employees' representatives are in a minority (though the balance may shortly be held by a third force acceptable to both sides). Often they are fairly easily overawed by the greater knowledge and experience of the representatives of management. Within the board of management, the workers have no direct representation and may only be partially represented by the labour manager, whose loyalty is usually primarily to the board rather than to the workers who have approved his appointment. And it is this mangement board which reaches the most essential decisions within the enterprise. The degree of control obtained by workers in this case is thus strictly limited.

In Sweden, a slightly different type of system has been established. Under agreements between the federations of employers and unions, a system of works councils has been established for every major industrial enterprise. Normally these councils have roughly equal numbers representing the workers and management, with additional representatives of salaried staff and supervisors. Representatives of employees are elected for two-year spells. Meetings take place quarterly. The main purpose of the meetings is the transmission of information. Management provides information on the present state of the market, the competitive and accounting position of the firm, proposed working changes and assessments of the likely consequence of this. Representatives of the employees may make suggestions and proposals on any of these matters, but there is no question of a veto. Proposals concerning manpower reductions or increases must at least have been discussed in the council before they can be implemented. Such councils operate not only in industry and commerce, but also in nationalised industries, the civil service and even the armed forces. Here too, however, though the councils probably establish a greater *sense* of involvement among employees (which is certainly important in itself), it does not appear, from their own account, that the workers have obtained any very effective influence over the main management decisions, even those concerning long-term policy.

In Israel, a system of joint consultation has been established, also by agreement between the trade union federation and the association of manufacturers. All enterprises employing more than fifty people must set up a joint production committee. Workers' representatives are elected from all employees (or occasionally are nominated by workers' committees which are similarly elected) and sit for a year in the first place. The joint production committees have two chairmen, one representing each side. They discuss certain aspects of pay and conditions, for example incentive schemes (though other aspects are decided by national agreements or by negotiation in the workers' committees), production problems generally, suggestions schemes, trading prospects and new projects of training and supervision. Outside experts may be brought in to assist the discussions if their presence is thought useful. In this case the committees may take executive decisions if representatives of management and workers agree, though in other cases their recommendations are only advisory. Here, therefore, though the basic system is one of consultation, rather than joint discussion and decision of major problems, workers may in appropriate cases exert some effective influence over management decisions.

Somewhat similar plans are now being discussed for Britain. It remains to be seen whether these will provide any more genuine sense of participation for workers than in the schemes already outlined. There have however already been experiments of this kind in Britain, which go further than anything described so far. The Glacier Metal Company, employing over 5000 people, has over many years implemented a system of this kind. Under this there is a clear constitution for the firm, under which workers' representatives express their views within a kind of legislature. In each factory or unit of the company there exists a council consisting of the chief executive of the enterprise, one representative of the senior staff, two of middle-level staff, three of clerical, and seven shop stewards. Thus shop-floor workers balance the rest, but the numbers are unimportant because the council operates on a system of veto, by which any one vote can prevent a decision being reached. The council meets once a month and other employees may attend as observers. A chairman is elected from outside the council. The subjects discussed include wages and salary structures, wage systems, hours of work, holidays, redundancy, factory closures, overtime, night shifts and changes in work methods. A clear distinction is drawn between participation in day-to-day management decisions and in the long.term programme and goal within whose framework those decisions are made. The council is concerned above all in the formulation of a written company policy document, which is modified from time to time, and with a series of 'standing orders', dealing with major matters affecting the company. These are made available to every employee in a printed loose-leaf book. Under the constitution every proposal to be adopted must receive unanimous consent. This could have meant that no change ever took place, but it is claimed that, both organisationally and technologically, the rate of change of the company has been high, and achieved without serious labour problems. It is said that so long as managers act within the framework of the agreed policy, their decisions receive the support of the workers' representatives and that indeed they will be criticised if they fail to act firmly and effectively. There has been no strike at the factory since 1936.[2]

The John Lewis organisation, established as a profit-sharing 'partnership' by the former owner, J. Spedan Lewis, operates in a similar way. The basic principle here is that all employees are owners of the firm, all equally being 'partners' in the organisation. The managers are in fact appointed in the same way as managers in other parts of industry, by promotion or by appointment by their superiors. They are, however, supposed to be accountable to the employees as a whole. Their duties and responsibilities are carefully laid down in the rules and regulations and changes in their functions could not be brought about without formal amendments of these. Control in the partnership is formally shared between the central council, the central board and the chairman. The council is a body of about 140 people, mainly elected by the entire workforce in branch constituencies of about 150 employees, but including also some representatives of the management. It meets only six or seven times a year, but work is conducted between-times by the standing committees which it elects. The council may amend the articles of association (though it needs the chairman's agreement), make recommendations on policy to the central board and the chairman, and in extreme circumstances dismiss the chairman. Perhaps more important in giving workers a sense of self-management are the large number of 'committees of communication', representing rank-and-file members, which meet regularly to discuss grievances within each department and any matters affecting their members, including suggestions concerning management. All the profits of the company which are not devoted to reinvestment are distributed to the partners as a bonus. The amount now represents about 15 per cent over and above wages or salaries, which are themselves rather higher than in comparable organisations elsewhere.[3]

A more thoroughgoing system of workers' control has been set up in Yugoslavia. Under this every enterprise in the country establishes its own workers' council. In firms of less than 30 employees all workers serve on the council. In larger enterprises the council is elected. The councils may have anything from 15 to 120 members and they meet monthly. They hold office for two years, and no member may serve more than twice in succession. More than 75 per cent of those elected are manual workers, the rest representatives of staff. The council appoints and dismisses the management board; it approves or rejects the plan for the enterprise, which sets out the general production and sales goals; and it makes decisions of principle concerning investment, the implementation of the plan and the running of the enterprise, including working hours, working conditions, engagements and dismissals. The management board which they elect, mainly from among their own number, is responsible for the execution of the plan approved, and for the appointment of all other senior staff. It meets much more frequently, at least once a week, reaches decisions on management matters and formulates proposals for the council, even on the annual plan, income schedules, etc. In large firms there may be a separate council for each department, branch, or 'economic unit'. Again most of the members are ordinary workers who continue in employment, and they too must resign after two years. Here the proportion of manual workers is rather lower. Some decisions of the workers' council require to be approved in addition by the trade unions, including the decisions concerning the allocation of the profits of the enterprise, and all decisions affecting wages. The enterprise is officially the property of the workers, who may sell part of its assets, merge or associate with other enterprises, raise loans for development from the bank. But the enterprise is not totally independent. It must work under the general oversight of the elected Economic Chamber (which in

1962 replaced chambers for different industries), and it is influenced by the fiscal and monetary controls exercised by the federal and republican governments. There are also some government controls over raw material prices and minimum wages.[6]

There have been some difficulties in operating this system. Sometimes the director finds himself in conflict with the workers' or management councils. He is entitled to refuse to implement decisions reached by them if he can show that they conflict with the law, or with other regulations of the government authorities. In some cases the conflict is only finally resolved by the dismissal of the director by the workers' council. Yet judged in terms of national economic interests the director may have been right. Because of these difficulties there has recently been a move towards according greater authority and autonomy to the manager, and restricting the degree of control exercised by the workers' council.

In considering such forms of organisation, one dilemma that arises is similar to one that occurs in the political field: is there a conflict between more efficiency and more democracy? And if so, what is the balance to be struck? There are obviously wide differences in the knowledge, experience and expertise available to workers on the one hand and to managers on the other. In a strictly economic sense, managers might reach 'better' decisions if left wholly to themselves. But they might also reach more unacceptable decisions, and so cause more problems later. With an ever more educated, self-conscious and independent workforce, managers can no longer expect to be able to impose decisions on their employees without consideration of their views. Moreover, economic efficiency is not necessarily the only criterion. Work-satisfaction is also important and will probably come to be regarded as more so in the future. Nor is efficiency *necessarily* prejudiced. If the issues are presented clearly enough, workers' representatives are probably well able to make a *choice* between two or three alternative choices. They have after all a common interest with management in increased efficiency. Thus their participation is unlikely to be a serious brake on productivity. Yet it may hugely increase their sense of commitment and their sense of satisfaction with their work.

The type of control demanded by employees is not necessarily of the same type demanded by managers. Workers are concerned, above all, about those questions which affect their working lives. This means they are concerned over long-term policy, above all over decisions that will affect employment prospects, about payments schemes, pensions, welfare benefits and others. These are also mainly the areas of which workers have most first-hand knowledge, and which they are best-equipped to discuss. It is on these questions therefore that the participation of workers is most badly required, and for these that it is best adapted. On many other questions, the introduction of a new marketing programme, the modification of the design of a product, or the details of new types of equipment, workers' representatives are usually less concerned. On these more technical questions about *means*, they will be more willing to accept expert guidance. Even here, they may have useful opinions and experience to offer. The essential point is that they feel they are consulted and involved.

But most of the systems we have looked at provide only a marginal sense of participation by workers' representatives. To provide a full sense of participation, the system must achieve more. As in the political field, one of the most vital requirements is that influence can be brought to bear at an early stage, well before final decisions are reached. 'Consultation' which merely consists in informing employees of a decision with little effective opportunity for influencing or reversing it is not consultation in any meaningful sense at all. This means that councils must have the means of acquiring all the information they require on the future plans and policies of management; and in particular that they are given the maximum possible advance notice of any proposed change which may affect employees' interests in an important way (the Central Electricity Generating Board in Britain gives at least a year's notice to its employees of the possibility of an impending closure of a power-station). It is the announcement of decisions already reached, over which he has had little influence, which most gives the worker the feeling of being without effective control over his work. He has the right to be well informed about the financial situation of the enterprise, its marketing and sales prospects and policies, labour turnover, engagements and dismissals, productivity and labour costs, training and apprenticeship schemes, and technical developments.

Secondly, to be effective, councils of this type must have effective *powers*. They must have real functions if they are not to be just talking-shops. They can themselves undertake the management or supervision of welfare facilities, canteens, conditions of work and other matters. They can supervise an appeals system to hear claims against arbitrary dismissal or unfair treatment. They can administer pension, sickness and other social security schemes. They can share in influencing investment and marketing decisions. Finally, they can provide something like a legislative system, by which the basic principles and purposes governing the enterprise and the main lines of policy can be laid down by those who work there. It is in this way above all that a sense of self-determination can be induced. This need not represent an unacceptable inhibition on the powers of management, nor need it prevent a company from having an extremely successful commercial record.[5]

However, even all this together would not solve the basic problem of 'alienation', the worker's sense of not being fully in control of his own economic destiny. This derives, as we have seen, in the economic field as in the political, above all from the scale of modern organisation. A representative council directing the affairs of a vast economic enterprise, having hundreds or even thousands of workers, will normally give the individual workers as little sense of control over his own affairs as corresponding, and equally remote, representative bodies in the political field. The most important requirement for a genuine sense of participation, therefore, is the establishment of representative bodies at a much lower level: this means not merely separate councils for each division or plant within an undertaking – it means there should be a committee for each shop-floor. Indeed, it can be argued that for practical purposes workers should be organised into groups of only ten or a dozen. These could have group production programmes and rewards. They could elect one of their number to be their representative on a shop-floor committee, to discuss matters affecting the entire shop-floor: this in turn could send representatives to works committees, and so on.

A representative system under which each and every worker would thus have not only an abstract right, but an easy *opportunity*, to exercise influence could do more than any other single measure to create the industrial democracy that has so often been discussed, but so rarely achieved: a system in which *every* worker has the chance to participate personally, and not just the favoured few who are elected to committees and council. It is this opportunity to exercise influence *directly*, at the work-place, that a socialist society must be most concerned to create.

7.4 *Socialist Ownership*

But even a system of full-scale workers' control over the enterprise would not solve the problem of socialist *ownership*.

Both in socialist and in capitalist states it is the system of control in industry which most closely affects the worker's life and so is most important to him. But this does not mean that the system of ownership is unimportant. The sense that the *ownership* of the enterprise in which he works is in wholly alien hands, though perhaps less immediately important than the sense that control is outside his influence, is none the less discouraging and illogical.

The vesting of ownership in capitalist states among the shareholders, most of whom never see the operations from one year to the next, is an anachronism. As we have just seen, the shareholder today is divorced from any effective share in control. He usually has little interest in or knowledge of the company at all. He contributes nothing to its success. He has merely bought a piece of paper from somebody else. He need take no action at all except refrain from selling his holding. Yet it is he, and he alone, who receives the variable reward which represents the fruits of the enterprise's success.

Nor can it really be said that the shareholder directs funds into the channels required by the economy. His purchase of a share provides no money for the company at all. It is true that it may make it easier for the enterprise to raise money in the future. But whether or not the money is raised depends on the judgement of managers and directors, not on the shareholders. Indeed, the main influence is in the opposite direction. The shareholder today cannot possess the knowledge or judgement to decide whether a particular investment project which a company proposes is or is not likely to be successful. He places his judgement in that of the directors who recommend it, not the reverse. But in any case, whether he buys a share will depend on his assessment of the views other shareholders are likely to take in the future, rather than his assessment of the project itself.

In any case most shareholders today are institutions of various kinds. Such institutions, insurance companies and pensions funds, are unwilling to invest their money in projects which carry a large element of risk. Nor, indeed, as we have seen, will most investment decisions anyway normally involve much element of risk. When very large sums of money are involved in each decision, there is even a case for saying there *should* be little risk: in a modern economy, when investment is large and lumpy, each venture should be carefully planned and calculated, so that the dangers of a faulty investment are largely removed. In this situation the case for according 'ownership' to those who provide funds, and thus for paying the shareholder a variable return as the payment for 'risk', is largely undermined.

Any risk which the shareholder undergoes is usually not related to the success of the enterprise so much as to the vagaries of the market. Most companies have assets of such size that they can withstand considerable trading losses for substantial periods. They are often so diversified that losses in one area can be made good elsewhere. In so far as their fortunes fluctuate, it is according to a *government's* general economic policies, or the state of world trade, rather than on anything which the company does itself. Where there are losses, a succession of poor dividends may be made good for the shareholder by capital appreciation (in Britain the periods between mid-1967 and mid-1968, and between the beginning and end of 1975, periods of depression and low dividends, saw a doubling of share values). Thus the essential justification for a high rate of return, even if variable from year to year – the risk of the total loss of his capital – is today largely removed.

Moreover, most money today is raised by internal savings or from the banks, rather than from the market. It is notable that the most successful capitalist economies of modern times, those of West Germany and Japan, rely hardly at all on the alleged venturesomeness of the private shareholder in risking his capital. Yet they succeed in raising money for business ventures and innovations quite as well – indeed far better – than Britain does. The private shareholder, the archetypal capitalist, the official owner, thus increasingly today loses much of his *raison d'être*. He becomes an irrelevance. He has no effective control or influence on the company, nor even an important financing role. He certainly contributes virtually nothing to its success or failure. This depends on the industriousness of the workers, on the skill of the management, above all on the government's management of the economy.

Yet the profits are appropriated exclusively by the shareholder who has contributed least to winning them. If anybody might expect a share in the profits, it is either the management or the workers, to whom success or failure might reasonably be attributed. These are those whose working lives are invested in the enterprises and whose stake in it is greatest. They may reasonably regard themselves as entitled to win the rewards which may be gained in periods of success. Conversely, they might also be prepared to forgo gains for the sake of the enterprise in periods of difficulty. They could reasonably be seen as holding the enterprise in their hands.

It would not be difficult to establish a system on these lines, corresponding far better with economic rationality and common sense alike. Under such a system ownership would be vested in the employees of the undertaking, and shareholdings transferred to them. Whatever dividend was earned (or not) in any individual year would now go to those whose successes (or inadequacies) had brought them into being. Other providers of capital, whether banks or debenture-holders, would receive only fixed interest payments; and they would become *creditors*, not owners. Such a system could be applied equally within socialist economies. Indeed it would be a form of microcosmic socialism far more relevant to workers' needs than the state socialism of recent years.

Under such a system a 'share' in the company and a share in the profits would be distributed roughly in accordance with the real share in, and contribution to, its activities each had had. An incentive would thus be provided, and a reward, for those most clearly and closely involved. A sense of commitment to the enterprise would be created among them. The traditional demand by socialists for 'common' ownership would be reconciled with the need for ownership by the *worker* of his own instruments of production; and for a form of ownership not so remote as to cause alienation. Far more genuinely than under state socialism today, the worker could feel himself to share in the *ownership* as well as the control of the enterprise in which he worked.

Under such a system ownership and control would once more be united in the same hands. And because both would now be diffused, the concentration of economic power which exists today in company boards, or state corporations, would be reduced. New centres of economic power – individual self-managed groups and enterprises – would be established at the grass-roots to counteract and challenge the power of the forces at the centre.

Socialism today, therefore, in an age when economic enterprises have become vast in scale, and when management and ownership have become as impersonal and remote under state socialism as under capitalism, must be concerned with the means of diffusing both ownership and control more widely. This means, on the one hand, the promotion of small-scale enterprise, or at least small-scale plants and units within large enterprises. On the other, and above all, it means vesting both ownership and control in those who work, and are most directly involved, within each enterprise.

Here too, the monopoly of power by the nation-state has distorted and deformed original socialist theory. If the ideals of socialism are to be genuinely achieved today, the idea of social ownership needs to take on quite a new meaning: the common ownership of individual workshops, establishments or enterprises by those who work in them and have the greatest stake in them. By their joint efforts, they may then be able to improve the performance of that enterprise and so their own rewards. Social ownership would acquire not only a new meaning but a real meaning: far more than the state socialism of today, such a system might be able to transform the existence of individual workers and secure for them a meaningful control over their own lives at work, as socialist thinkers have always dreamed.

8 Inequality in Wealth

8.1 *Justifications for Inequalities in Wealth*

But it is not only over the distribution of political and economic power that socialists have been concerned. They are also concerned, and even more fundamentally, about the distribution of wealth.

However much influence, whether economic or political, becomes more equally diffused, however much income itself is equalised, this may be only temporary in effect, so long as there remain widespread disparities in wealth itself.

There is one obvious and fundamental difference in kind about income from wealth. Income deriving from employment, however unequal it may be, is all related, directly or indirectly, to the actions of the individuals who receive it: at least in theory reward can be related roughly to effort. Where wealth has been acquired by its *present* owner, this too may result from his own efforts. But where it has been bequeathed or given, as in most cases, income from property derives from the acts of others. The recipient himself has contributed nothing at all to its acquisition. The important distinction to be made, therefore, is not so much between work-income and property-income, 'earned' and 'unearned' income (though this too is important), but between property income that is self-acquired and property-income that has been inherited.

A very large proportion of the highest fortunes in Britain and similar states at present are still acquired by inheritance. And in other cases large sums are transferred before death. Inequality of this kind is therefore one that is transmitted from one generation to the next. It is quite outside the control of the recipients. Personal wealth is still concentrated in relatively few hands, despite the effects of death duties, inheritance tax, taxation on unearned income and capital transfer taxes.

But property-income of this type may provide a substantial additional income, as high or even higher than income from employment. Moreover capital assets may themselves *appreciate* in value, sometimes very rapidly indeed. In Britain equities roughly doubled in value in 1958 and 1959, and more than doubled during 1975 alone without their owners being obliged to do anything whatsoever except watch their assets double. Between 1945 and 1960, gross dividends from the shares included in the *Financial Times* index grew by more than three times, and the capital value grew by nearly three times.[1] Capital gains of this type may be used either to provide still further income or still more capital gains. Moreover in considering rises in personal wealth, one should also include rises in *undistributed* profits (which remain the property of shareholders and are a form of deferred income).[2] Whether property is held in equities, in housing and pictures, or in other forms, it will still make available steep increases in wealth not available to those who own no property.

A number of justifications have been found in defence of property-income. One is that it is a reward for saving, or for the abstinence which saving involves. But under this argument, such rewards should be payable only to those who had themselves undertaken the saving, not to those who merely receive other people's savings: it is therefore scarcely relevant to the case of inherited property. Again, though this argument might conceivably justify a regular *interest* payment for savers, it hardly supports the huge gains acquired in capital appreciation as well. Finally, even for those who have saved themselves, there is in fact no close relationship between saving and abstinence. Those living on high incomes can save with little or no effort, almost automatically – certainly without conspicuously abstaining. But those on small incomes, with a family to support, save only with the utmost sacrifice. If rewards were really to be given for effort or abstinence, savings by the latter would require a far higher reward than those by the former.

Property-income is also sometimes justified in terms of the value to the economy as a whole of high savings: as an *incentive* rather than a reward. But there is very little evidence that the willingness to save is influenced by the rate of interest that may be obtained. If no interest at all were to be paid, savings would no doubt decline, but short of this, changes in interest rates do not seem to exert great influence on the volume saved. The Radcliffe report on the monetary system in Britain expressed marked scepticism towards the idea that the rate of interest was a factor governing the rate of saving. It noted that 'witnesses concerned with the National Savings Movement . . . when it came to encouraging the habit of saving . . . emphasised anything but the rate of interest,'[3] Moreover, today the greater part of savings is undertaken by corporations, insurance companies, investment funds and others, for which the rate of interest, though significant, is marginal: such bodies have no alternative to saving anyway, other than giving their wealth away. The chance of capital gains is probably a more important incentive, for both personal and institutional investors. But the fact that there continues to be demand for fixed-interest stocks shows that it is not an essential one. People save partly merely as a means of reserving purchasing-power for the future: indeed a considerable amount might take place anyway for this purpose, even if there were little reward either in income or in capital gains.

Finally, some kinds of property-income, mainly that from shares, are justified on grounds of *risk*. But, as we saw in the last chapter, there is normally now only marginal risk involved in such investments. And in very large-scale undertakings it is doubtful how much investment should involve risk.

But even if the right to enjoy a reward for saving were on these grounds accepted, this would still not apply to inherited property. This is sometimes justified in terms of the right of individuals to provide, through their own efforts, not only for themselves, but for their children, grandchildren and other dependants and relations. However little this wealth may have been earned, or deserved, by those who subsequently *receive* it, it is claimed, the right to *give* has been earned by those who bequeath it. It is argued that this is as important an incentive to save as the desire for capital for personal use.

There is, here, a genuine choice to be made between the right of one generation to transmit their savings, and the right of another to start on roughly equal terms. It can reasonably be argued that the latter is by far the more important right. The right to transmit property carried considerable weight in earlier times, when the responsibility of family ancestors and the importance of blood ties loomed larger than they do today, and when dependants were more, and more permanently, dependent than they are today. That right has already been eroded by the taxation of property and inheritance which has long taken place. The greatest needs of dependants are anyway usually felt while the bequeather is still alive. Most people's children are forty or fifty by the time they die, and may have been generously assisted in their youth. Widows can be assisted by insurance and other provisions. Today the demand for equal starting-points would therefore probably carry greater weight.

However, as in the case of income, the most important point is to examine *where* the main differences in wealth occur. Today, though inequalities in wealth among individuals within states remain wide, they are far less so than the inequalities in wealth between *states* (and therefore between individuals in different states). It is here above all that the process of accumulation, in this case collective accumulation – the saving of groups rather than individuals – has produced the most glaring inequalities. It is here that inheritance is today most crucial in effect: the inheritance by enterprises and communities, as well as individuals, of the wealth stored up in the past. And while the inheritance of individuals can be taxed, so as to reduce the resulting inequalities, this is impossible in the case of the inheritance of collective wealth. It is these inequalities in *collective* wealth that are most important in their effect today.

Socialists who are concerned to reduce inequalities in wealth, therefore, must be concerned specially about the means of overcoming the widest differences in property which exist today: those between the collectivities to which people belong all over the world.

8.2 *The Redistribution of Wealth*

If inequalities in wealth are so important, what are the ways in which they can be reduced?

Within states a number of ways have been used for this purpose over the years. One marginal measure has been taxation of 'unearned' income, that is income derived from wealth, at a higher rate than income derived from work. But such taxes leave most of such income intact and certainly do not deter a rapid accumulation of property from still taking place. Moreover, such taxes on income cannot prevent the emergence of still greater inequalities (and further acquisition of wealth) through rapid capital gains.

For this reason taxes on income are normally today accompanied by the taxation of capital gains. Capital gains today are often the main source of rapid accumulation of wealth, and they can completely distort the redistributive effect of other taxation. For the US, for example, the effect of capital gains is virtually to eliminate the progressive effect which taxation on income achieves.[4] In Britain the tax on such gains is so low that it does not significantly slow the rate of accumulation. In the high-growth inflationary economies of the post-war world, these gains, though occasionally checked, or even reversed, for a year or two, have become an important factor in changing the distribution of wealth, between holders of shares and holders of government stocks, as well as between the wealthy and the non-wealthy. They would need much more drastic checking if inequality in wealth is not to go on increasing in Western states today.

Far more important in affecting the distribution of wealth is the taxation of inheritance. Taxes on inheritance should logically be levied, not on estates, or those who bequeath, as is often the case today, but on those who receive. The social aim of such taxes is to restrict the differential advantages accruing to individuals through the chance of inheritance, not to restrict the amount any individual may *leave* at death. To levy on recipients would encourage the wealthy to disperse their property more widely. The legatee, conversely, should be taxed more highly if he had received other legacies. Any tax of this kind, if it is to be effective, must clearly be accompanied by similar measures to tax gifts among the living, not only in the last few years before their death, but at any age: otherwise the whole purpose of the legislation can be frustrated by making over property some years before death. Thus, since the object is to secure greater equality in personal wealth, any such tax must apply to all wealth transferred by gift as well as by bequest, not merely that transferred at death or just before.[5]

But many of these taxes are already applied in many Western societies. And they have so far largely failed to exert any significant effect on the distribution of wealth, and so on the income associated with it. High levels of income today, moreover, make it possible for very large personal properties to be *acquired*, even without inheritance. If differences in property are to be reduced, therefore, there is clearly need in addition for some form of graduated levy on existing capital, under which inequalities in wealth itself could be reduced. Levies on wealth are, it is true, expensive to collect. But this difficulty has been overcome in Sweden and other countries where such a tax has been levied regularly. And if any real and visible impact is to be made on the vast disparities of wealth that exist within modern Western societies, it may be (until greater equality of income is achieved) only through the use of some such measures.

But possibly more important than to take away wealth from those who have it is to redistribute it to those who do not.

As we saw in the last chapter, the joint-stock company system, as it operates in many states today, concentrates *ownership* of each company, and in theory ultimate control, in the hands of shareholders who in practice take no day-to-day part in its affairs, and in most cases know little about its operations. For this reason those shareholders enjoy exclusive right to the profits earned by the enterprise, though their efforts have normally contributed little or nothing to its success. They secure that right by the buying of a piece of paper, regardless of the fact that this transaction normally injects no new money whatever into the company concerned. The inequality in ownership reflects and reinforces inequalities in wealth.

Such a shareholder's interest is not in the enterprise itself, but in the piece of paper and in the revenue which it may bring (or, more likely, the increased price he may be able to get by selling it at some time in the future). His decision to dispose of the piece of paper depends not on what will benefit the company, but what will benefit himself; and his success in that transaction will depend not on anything which he contributes to the company, but on his ability to foresee its success—or more accurately, his ability to foresee the calculations made by others of its success. He could indeed perhaps be described as a fortune-teller, who earns exceptionally high fees for successful predictions (but one who contributes nothing at all to the economic performance of the country or the enterprise in doing so).

The position is very little different for the relatively few shareholders who may have bought the original shares when issued and have held on to their holding. Their interest in the enterprise is little greater. They too will have little personal knowledge of its operations. They too will probably dispose of their holding at any moment they regard as favourable to the seller rather than the enterprise: indeed it is when the enterprise is in greatest difficulty and most needs their help that they will be most disposed to sell. And though they have indeed, in this case, provided capital for the undertaking, the risks of doing so, as we saw earlier, may have been minimal in relation to the probability of income and capital gain. For they find themselves in the fortunate (if inexplicable) situation where, when the management makes a successful production decision or marketing venture, or when the workers make particularly strenuous efforts to improve their rate of production, the benefit accrues not to those who undertake these actions but to themselves.

It is perhaps only the essential passivity of human nature which has allowed such an illogical system to continue with so little protest or even perplexity. Even socialists, who have long denounced the private ownership of the means of production, and who might therefore be expected to be the most indignant, show themselves remarkably tolerant of that illogicality. Yet it is that system (not only making the distribution of ownership of the means of production highly unequal, but allowing the continued transmission of that absentee ownership from one generation to the next) which is largely responsible for existing inequalities in property and so in wealth.

It would not in fact be difficult to introduce changes which would reduce the illogicality of the current situation, and at the same time do much to equalise the privilege of property ownership in each state. For if it is illogical that individuals who never see an enterprise and never go near it, and contribute nothing to its success, should be regarded as its owners, it is almost equally mystifying that those who do go near it, who spend their lives within it, and whose efforts determine its success or failure are held to have no share in owning it. They have invested their labour and their livelihood in the undertaking and are infinitely more involved in its activities than the shareholders. But because they have invested no cash, they are held to be disinterested outsiders, who have no claim on the means of their livelihood and must accept any decision that might be made by the 'owners', even if this means that they are discharged from the company's affairs at a week's notice and returned to the dole queue. Both logic and social justice, as was indicated in the last chapter, suggest that it is these, who have the largest personal stake in the enterprise, who should be regarded as 'owners', and it is they who should therefore draw the differential rewards resulting from relative success or failure in any one year.

The simplest and most painless way of achieving this goal would be by a measure demanding a progressive transfer of 'shares' in all

joint-stock enterprises to those who worked within each company.
Eventually each would thus become a co-operative undertaking
whose ownership was vested in those who work in it. It would then
be for each enterprise to decide, on the basis of the employees'
decision, whether or not they wished to raise capital in the future
on the market, or from banks, finance houses and other institutional sources; and if so, whether any of those who provided
capital should be rewarded through variable payments or only
through the payment of fixed interest. Conversely they could
decide how far they themselves would be willing to contribute,
either through immediate payments, or through the deferment of
salaries and wages, to its capital needs. Many employees might
well decide that they would rely on fixed-interest borrowing to
meet their external needs and finance, while those within the
enterprise itself would carry the risks of the variable interest
charge. In either case it would be primarily the employees who,
through the distribution of shares, or through regular bonus
payments, would benefit (or suffer) from year to year according to
the fortunes of the enterprise. And wealth would be diversified.

But all these steps together would not prevent inequalities from
re-emerging unless effective measures are taken to level inequalities in incomes themselves. For it is the wide disparity in incomes,
allowing differential rates of saving, which is generally responsible
for wide disparities in wealth. This makes possible, as we saw,
saving on quite unequal terms. If *incomes* were more equal,
therefore, and the terms of saving so made more equivalent, and
inherited wealth taxed more heavily, the minor differences in
property that might still result would seem more acceptable.

8.3 *Collective Wealth*

As we saw earlier, however, increasingly the main source of
inequality in wealth today is inequality in *collective* wealth; above
all that between the wealth of different localities and states.

One form this takes is the collective wealth of enterprises
themselves. Some are profitable and expanding, some are unprofit-
able and declining. To some extent how far they are profitable
may be outside the control of those who work within them:
dependent on the market, tariff decisions, changing tastes and
fashion. The system we have just described, under which workers

shared more genuinely and directly in the success of their own enterprise, would not in itself necessarily secure justice between employees in *different* industries. The worker in the computer company might expect a rich dividend or bonus every year, while the one in the struggling textile firm, or the subsidised transport undertaking, might expect nothing. Here it is only through the tax system of the state (or the region or locality) that the inequalities could be evened out, so providing relatively equal chances for different types of enterprise to earn a surplus for redistribution.

More significant are the collective inequalities between regions within the same state. These may have the effect that a share in the enterprise for workers in one region (say in the south of Italy or the north-east of Britain) would be worth far less than a share in some other region (say in the north of Italy or the south of Britain). In other words particular conditions of the region as a whole – its geographical situation, its poor communications, its inadequate infrastructure, its deficient markets – may affect the conditions of competition for all enterprises (and therefore the owners of enterprises, their workers). Here too it is only through taxation and comparable measures that such inequalities could be allowed for and redressed. Differential taxes can be levied, special tax allowances and rates of depreciation may be offered to the enterprises in the depressed regions, subsidies, employment premiums and other regional grants offered, so that the natural disadvantages would be, to some extent at least, compensated by the artificial assistance offered by the government concerned.

Far more important than either of these, however, are the collective inequalities between states. For if the ownership of wealth is unevenly divided between individuals within states, and even between regions within states, it is far more unevenly shared between states themselves.

There are a number of reasons why this has become the most important collective inequality today. National economies developed, until relatively recently, largely independently and at varying rates. Industrialisation began at different periods for each of them, and therefore the process of accumulation and investment has been taking place for widely varying lengths of time. In addition, even when the time-scale has been similar, there have been large variations between them in terms of available raw materials, in the rates of investment, the success of investment, the social and political conditions, the degree and skill of government intervention, and so in the rate of economic growth achieved. As a result the wealth built up over the years in different states has varied even more than the wealth accumulated by different individuals within states. Yet while the inequalities in wealth among individuals can be redressed through taxation, there is no system of taxation which can redress the inequalities in wealth, especially in industrial property, between states.

In recent years, in particular, there have been other developments which have added to this differential rate of growth among collectivities. There is an increase in the amount of investment which is either financed by the internal savings of companies[6] or undertaken by governments. One effect of this is that the providers of capital and those who use it are now usually one and the same. While the old-fashioned enterpriser with funds at his disposal would make use of his funds for whatever venture he felt would be profitable, in any industry and any country, today, as we saw in Chapter 7, the company will invest mainly in itself, in traditional activities and in its own nation. This means that the distribution of investment is to a considerable extent determined by the distribution of savings: that is, by the distribution of *existing* production.

It is not that ventures in new fields are never considered, but *preference* will always be shown to ventures in familiar fields and regions. This is intensified because the direction of research and innovation too is determined by the distribution of previous success. It is mainly the large companies, which have enjoyed such success, and the already developed nations that can finance it. Not only money but know-how is distributed according to past successes. This too has the effect that the collective inequalities between enterprises, regions and nations are intensified.

Thus collective accumulation and collective investment produce large differences not only in current income but in wealth as well. Prosperous industries or enterprises can afford more new investment, more research, more advertising, better control of demand, and so can largely assure continued expansion. Similarly wealthy regions within states can afford more new investment, provide better public amenities, and a greater prospect of long-term prosperity than poor areas. Above all, wealthy countries can undertake more investment, more education, more research, and so assure themselves more wealth in the future. It is this which, in an increasingly integrated international community, is the chief and most crucial political consequence of collective accumulation and investment. While in earlier times the individual would distribute his personal savings all over the world (in Britain before the First World War half the total investment was abroad), today the state corporation, the local authority and the government will invest their savings only at home. So existing inequalities in wealth are magnified.

8.4 *The International Distribution of Wealth*

While the other collective inequalities of wealth, therefore, between enterprises and between regions, can be at least partly redressed through taxation and other measures, inequalities between the wealth of different states cannot be remedied in that way. There exists at present no international authority that can bring about the type of redistribution required. It is here that the existing domination of the national state is most powerful in its effect: while within the territories each controls it may be the instrument for reducing inequalities, within the world community national states become the instrument for magnifying inequalities.

There are no natural economic forces which serve to counteract the trend. In days gone by, private investment sought out those areas, often in foreign countries, where local funds were least, and where foreign investment might therefore be profitable. So British and US capital financed much of the infrastructure of Latin America, so European capital exploited the mineral and food resources of developing regions in Asia and Africa. In the process capital funds were made available to regions where few could be generated locally, and yet where labour costs were low and production potential available. Today, that process is only marginal in effect. Primary production, in which private investment mainly took place, now represents a far smaller proportion of total world production and world trade. Investment is increasingly concentrated in the manufacture of complex and sophisticated products, vehicles, planes, electronics, computers, machine tools, and other types of equipment. This is undertaken in the rich countries themselves, rather than abroad. For these the advantages of low labour costs are outweighed by the lack of local skills, and especially the lack of local markets.[7] So though IBM and ICI and many comparable corporations operate worldwide, though the transnational company becomes a far more powerful economic force than ever before, they are primarily selling home-produced goods to other lands, and investment is therefore now concentrated above all at home. Partly for this reason, trade and investment increases much more rapidly between rich countries than between rich countries and poor. It is now among the rich themselves that new wealth is mainly created and hoarded.

Occasionally there are sudden and dramatic changes in the terms of trade for particular products, as when the oil price suddenly multiplied by four or five in 1973/74. The effect of this was to transfer wealth (and therefore investment) on a large scale to countries previously poor in investment resources. But this benefited only a small minority of poor countries, while the rest were made even worse off than before. For, though the new rich were relatively generous in their provision of aid, that aid still only amounted to less than half of the increased costs which resulted for other poor countries as a result of the rise in the price. All that really occurred therefore was that a particular group of countries, which were not even among the poor before, were transformed to the category of very rich, while the genuinely poor became poorer. The basic balance between rich and poor was unchanged. The poorness of the poor, and their failure to attract investment resources as a result, was in no way affected: indeed it became even greater than before.

Nor has international aid done more than scratch the surface of the problem. In so far as the aid is genuinely aid, in so far, that is, as it takes the form of outright grants, or at least is at nil or reduced rates of interest, it does represent a real transfer of resources from rich countries to poor. But in so far as it is lent at market rates of interest, as is a great deal of 'aid', it does not have this effect at all. The interest payments of subsequent years reduce the wealth of poor countries, and increase that of rich, to an extent which often outbalances the initial transfer of resources from one to the other. Where the aid is tied, as most is, it compels the recipient to buy from a particular source. Nor is there any indication that the scale of genuine aid, or true transfer of resources, is likely in the foreseeable future to be at a rate that will even begin to alter the existing unbalanced distribution of this wealth, still less transfer it at a rate which can significantly alter the production of wealth in the future.

At present the long-term rates of growth of poor countries are as great as those of rich countries, and in some cases slightly greater, so far as national income as a whole is concerned. But their rate of growth per head is in nearly all cases slower, because of the higher rate of population growth. The important point, however, is that even if this ceased to be true, even if the rate of growth *per head* became the same, inequalities would continue to increase, and at a very rapid rate. A 4 per cent growth in income a head for the US means a growth of 300 dollars a year in the standard of living of each inhabitant of the US. An equivalent rate of growth in income per head in India gives a rise of a little over four dollars in the standard of living of each. In other words, even when an equal rate of growth is reached between the two groups of countries, inequality in absolute terms will still be becoming rapidly greater. And even if a slightly higher rate of growth in income a head was attained in poor countries, it would take many centuries before anything like an equal distribution in income was reached; and still more before the distribution of wealth, of accumulated income, was significantly affected.

We will consider in the last chapter of this book some of the ways in which this problem might be tackled. For the moment, however, we should recognise the radical challenge which these facts inevitably present to the traditional concepts of socialism. Socialism has been above all concerned about the injustices resulting from the existing distribution of private property; and it has sought to see the establishment of social ownership as the means of bringing about a greater equality, both in economic power and in monetary income. But the extension of social ownership within states – of state socialism – can only secure greater equality in these respects within states (and then, as we have seen, only if undertaken in the right way). It cannot do so between them.

If socialists remain concerned, therefore, with a just distribution of wealth and welfare in the world as a whole, they must acknowledge that it can be achieved today only through quite a different application of their traditional beliefs – in other words, through a different form of socialism – from that which has been traditionally proclaimed.

Part III: A New Socialism

9 Socialism at the Grass-roots: Community Socialism

9.1 *New Ends and New Means*

We have been concerned in this book with major changes within contemporary societies which have affected traditional ideas of socialism.

The first of these is the perpetual increase in the scale of organisation. This results at root from improvements in the system of communications. It affects every field of human existence. Even at the most basic level – the unit of habitation – villages are replaced by towns, and towns by large cities. In administration, the areas over which authority is exercised become greater all the time: local government areas are enlarged, more functions are taken over by the bigger authorities, above all, national governments take continually growing powers, intervening in an ever-wider range of ever more detailed and technical questions. In commerce and industry equally, mergers, take-overs and natural expansion lead towards larger and larger organisations, within which the individual worker feels himself an insignificant cog, without influence or status. And in both fields, the scale of organisation increasingly becomes international rather than national. Each change in technology increases the size of every organisation in which men work and raises still further the remoteness and inflexibility of authority.

A parallel trend derives from the development of communications in a different sense: the growth of new means of transmitting ideas and influence, especially the mass media. The effect is that a far larger number of people are subjected to similar influences deriving from a very small number of sources. The role of parents and family in education and upbringing becomes less strong in relation to that of school and peer-groups. Upbringing increasingly becomes public rather than private. The development of state systems of education, and its extension over ten or twelve years, from early childhood to adulthood, has the effect of conditioning people more deeply and more consistently in the values, attitudes and even the opinions that are approved within that society. Moreover, and perhaps more important, the influences that mould children become similar not only within any given nation but even between them. The many diverse cultures and traditions which flourished even until the last fifty years are today increasingly submerged by the single universal culture of modern civilisation. While the total number of influences to which each person becomes subject may be larger than ever before, these influences themselves become increasingly similar to each other.

In considering the possibility of alternative forms of organisation, it is necessary to consider first: how far are those trends *inevitable* results of changes in communications and technology? How far in other words *can* they be counteracted, even if desired?

Since some of the trends we have noted result from changes in the communications system, the first question is whether the latter could be reversed. It is difficult to see how changes in the *capability* of communication could be undone, even if this was desired. There are virtually no cases in history of technical advances being reversed or forgotten, even deliberately. Moreover, there are many clear material benefits resulting from improved communication which many would be reluctant to forgo, even if it was accepted that they inevitably had adverse *social* consequences.

But the persistence of the present techniques of *communication* does not necessarily mean that the trend to large-scale *organisation* must continue. In certain fields, it is true, the trend towards increased co-ordination and control, at wider and wider levels, is almost certain to go on. At the world level, the common interest in peace and security, in spreading the benefits of economic development, and in reducing conflict and waste in many functional fields, will continue to promote this tendency, and even to intensify it (see Chapter 10 below). Even within states the trend must be expected to continue in certain areas. In some fields however it may be that greater consciousness of the impoverishing effect of assimilation and centralisation may create countervailing forces: bring a greater concern to establish the maximum autonomy and independence for local units. For the key question is: even where increased scale, or increased co-ordination, or both, continue, how far need this in turn entail increased subordination, whether for groups or individuals? How far, conversely, are there some areas where the advantages to be gained in this way should be deliberately sacrificed, to preserve greater diversity, independence and spontaneity? Which are the goals that are truly 'common', and to such an extent that men must be prepared to sacrifice independence for material convenience? And which are those where the social benefit from co-ordination is outweighed by the *individual's* interest in spontaneity and diversity?

One of the most widely pursued common goals of recent times has been economic growth, which is generally regarded as the most important ambition of states. These pressures to high rates of growth not only endanger the world's resources but do not even procure the material satisfactions they are intended to provide. For the effect of competition is that high rates of growth can be achieved only by high rates of investment designed to secure higher productivity. This secures equivalent production with more equipment but less labour. Thus more and more people are displaced from their jobs who cannot necessarily find alternative employment in service industries or elsewhere. All over the Western world, in shipbuilding, in steel, in motor manufacture, in textiles, in fishing, in agriculture and other industries, employment rapidly declines. So the total number of those unemployed increases in all industrial countries and remains high even in those where a relatively high rate of growth is being achieved. And the very fact of high unemployment, by reducing total demand, lowers the level of investment and growth for the future. Periods of growth become shorter and those of recession become longer. The relatively simple devices for stimulating growth in earlier times – lower interest rates, budgetary deficits, fiscal expansion and public works – are either not attempted through fear of inflation, or if attempted do not achieve their effect. Despite persistent recession inflation remains strong, partly because of excessive increases in income obtained by those still at work, partly because of the large sections of the economy which are in public hands and are unaffected by anti-inflationary measures. Modern industrial societies, therefore, in appearance so advanced, are yet characterised by the bizarre spectacle of large sections of the population being without work, while ever higher levels of investment are undertaken to reduce employment still further in the future, so ensuring that the benefits of high growth are enjoyed by fewer and fewer people. Only some form of disarmament in investment all over the world, designed to ensure that increased production is secured by higher employment rather than ever-increasing levels of productivity, could overcome this problem and create economies run for the sake of people rather than things.

So long as growth remains the most highly valued common goal in most societies a considerable degree of central planning, large-scale organisation and restriction of individual freedom has to be accepted for the sake of achieving it. Similarly, for the sake of 'efficiency' in functional fields – ensuring that the principal administrative tasks, the running of the welfare state, the preservation of law and order, and other goals are fulfilled as economically as possible – the same price has been thought worth paying. Finally, as a means of securing a more 'just' society, with redistribution from more fortunate to less fortunate, the process of centralisation and authoritarian control has also been accepted: indeed, given the glaring injustices that remain, especially between states, it is likely that intervention for this purpose will increase rather than decline.

It may be that once a minimum achievement has been secured in each of these fields, they will cease to be the central aim of political endeavour. Men will then concern themselves with new goals, relating to non-material rather than material satisfaction, the more intimate community rather than national states or world society. But even while the older aims remain dominant, some change in the *means* of attaining them could be pursued. For the question is not only *whether* they should still be sought: but *how* they may be sought with least infringement of the individuality, spontaneity and freedom of society's individual members. Even where the trends towards organisation and mass communications we have noted continue, how can we reduce the regulating, standardising, side-effects which they at present bring in their train?

9.2 *The reversal of the spiral*

What type of political or social action then could reverse the trends to centralisation?

Let us first be clear what are the aspects of centralisation and scale that are most damaging to human creativity and human satisfaction.

There is nothing in modern industrial technology as such, or even in large-scale administrative structures, which must inevitably crush all human satisfactions. The drudgery or monotony or

unpleasantness of work is not *necessarily* greater in large administrative or economic structures than it is in small-scale ones. Large
organisations can often provide pleasanter and freer working
conditions. The modern office clerk in a large corporation, the
worker in a large industrial enterprise, usually has at least a more
attractive working environment than his contemporary in small
organisations, or than his predecessors in less highly organised
ages. Assembly-line work in industry can be *less* enslaving, *because* it
is more repetitive, than older forms of manual work: anybody who
has done it knows that one of its greatest merits is that it leaves the
mind comparatively free for other things.

Moreover, its higher productive capacity means large-scale
organisation also provides the means for more satisfying and richer
existence than ever before: above all for far more leisure. To
attempt to turn the clock back, to return to the spinning-wheel and
the ox, to abandon altogether modern industrial techniques (as
attempted so unsuccessfully by Ruskin, Tolstoy, Gandhi and other
visionaries in earlier times) would be only a deluded and doomed
attempt to hold back the future. Here history has a clear lesson:
what works will win. Any technology which cheapens production
is likely to prevail eventually. The immediate advantages such
technology can afford are so manifest, the pressures of competition
(national as well as commercial) in their favour so powerful, that
Luddite creeds are no more likely to prevail today than in former
times.

Thus to attribute the dissatisfactions of modern Western man, as
do some contemporary writers, to 'industrial civilisation', or
'industrial technology', is a form of romanticism which conceals a
faulty appreciation of the true source of discontent. This applies
even more to currently fashionable denunciations of the 'consumer
society', which have even less intellectual substance. So long as
people have material needs or wants at all, they will be consumers.
No one is obliged in any society to consume more than he wishes. It
is the pressure of advertising, which may lay undue emphasis on
consumption and so increase wants, not the wants themselves,
which may justly be condemned (for this reason there are strong
grounds, on aesthetic as much as on economic and sociological
grounds, for far heavier taxation of advertising expenditure than at
present). If this is the objection, the denunciation should more
logically be not of the 'consumer' society, but of the 'commercial'
society.

It is not so much modern industry or technology that should be attacked but the *organisation* of modern industry and large-scale administration. What is really at fault is the lack of scope for spontaneity or originality in work, the oppressive character of the organisation's all-pervading influence, the remoteness of authority and its imperviousness to influence, the difficulty of obtaining promotion or recognition, the dependence of the worker on the organisation for welfare, pension, promotion and continued prospects, the moulding of attitudes by the ethos of the state or the firm, and other aspects. It is these that are dehumanising; it is these that can be said to degrade modern work when compared to that of the independent peasant proprietor tilling the fields, or the craftsman shaping his own products. The real problem for modern man therefore is not how to do away with large-scale organisation altogether, but how to enjoy some of its benefits without submitting to the slavery it can impose when allowed to rule unchecked.

If the danger of centralisation is that it creates excessive subordination, alienation and uniformity, one obvious remedy is deliberately to decentralise, to break up the organisation, to provide the maximum autonomy for its sub-units; and so to maintain, promote and encourage the maximum possible *diversity*. If large-scale organisation, political and economic, threatens to impose external goals on the individuals who are caught up in it, the clear solution is to provide the widest possible opportunity for sub-units to influence those goals. Finally, if the techniques of modern education, communications and child-rearing instil standardised and uniform attitudes, opinions and even personality, what is needed is deliberate effort to encourage diversity in all these fields to counteract those tendencies.

It is by these means therefore that the existing spiral may be reversed. It is equally by these means that the original ideals of socialism may be attained: a genuine sharing of ownership and control of the tools of work by those who use them, a true sense for the worker of control over his own destiny, a more free and democratic form of social organisation. If these ideals are to be achieved it will only be at a lower level of organisation: when socialism returns where it belongs – to the community within which the human being lives and works.

9.3 *Community Socialism*

This aim – to encourage small-scale organisations, local units, community sentiments, to intensify the upward movements within society against the downward ones – can be achieved only through a deliberate and determined effort. All the *natural* forces at present are in the reverse direction. The concentration of power at the top, and in the state in particular, which we noted in the early chapters of this book, means that those who exercise power at that level have a built-in interest in maintaining the downward movements, and that they possess in their hands the means of maintaining them. They will do this not for selfish and personal ends, but to secure the goals and aspirations, the more efficient organisation of human affairs, that they believe necessary for society as a whole.

But even if they believe it to be in the interests of society, rather than of themselves, what they do serves the interests of society only in the way that *they*, from their vantage-point, at the apex of the organisation, believe to be desirable. They may well be applauded and supported in this view by large sections of the population indoctrinated with the same attitude. But that vision of society, seen from the top, in terms of the downward-moving initiatives required to order it still more minutely, is quite different from the vision from below, the view of what might seem desirable to *individual* persons and groups, taking the aspirations of their own small units or of individual human beings themselves as the measuring-rod.

This dilemma, the difficulty of promoting the upward movements against the downward ones, is a particularly serious one for the socialist state. So long as socialist belief is tied to the concept of state socialism, of the state as the natural agent of all social goals, demanding the continual strengthening of state ownership, state social services and state institutions of every kind, it is committed to strengthening the downwards movement. The debasement of socialism which took place when it was tied to the concept of state power here takes its most costly toll. Only if socialism can be geared to new forms of social consciousness, social responsibility, social action and social ownership, based on the small-scale society, the genuine *community*, will socialist aspirations be allied once more to the upward-moving rather than the downward-moving forces.

The first requirement is to develop the concept of socialism *at the grass-roots*: of social ownership and socialist organisation on a small scale, in the local unit; in the municipality rather than the state, the enterprise, or even the workshop, rather than the national industry; in the school, the housing association, the community centre, rather than in the society as a whole.

The concept of *sharing*, of common ownership, of common policies jointly agreed by all who participate, makes quite as much sense – indeed far more sense – in each of these contexts than it does in the framework of the state, where it has mainly been applied in recent years. The socialist city or small town, where a number of local undertakings, commercial and industrial, are run jointly, in the interests of the inhabitants as a whole, is more meaningful, in terms of achieving a sense of common aspiration, common ownership and common endeavour, than is the socialist state. Indeed it is arguable that the *neighbourhood* is a more suitable unit even than the city for this purpose. The jointly-run *neighbourhood* laundry, the neighbourhood bakery, the neighbourhood hairdresser, run not for private profit but for the equal benefit of all who live within the neighbourhood, might give some *genuine* sense of participation, of sharing, such as has not been provided by most public undertakings until now. It is not impossible to conceive of neighbourhood meetings open to all residents, at which the policies of the neighbourhood cinema, laundry or village store (as much as the cemetery or cricket team) are discussed. Ownership in this form would give a more meaningful share of control to the public, said to be the owners, and would more genuinely correspond with social sentiments and loyalties, than public ownership of the traditional kind under which the local bakery is one unit in a vast national chain. It is even possible that many would be willing to pay 2p a loaf more for real, crisp, locally-baked bread, sold close at hand, in their own bakery, than for soggy, nationally manufactured, steam-baked bread, sold at the city supermarket. 'Efficiency' would, in such a society, cease to be the sole criterion of organisation.

Similarly, in industry, when the individual small-scale enterprise is the autonomous unit, owned by, and ultimately controlled by, those who work within it, the sense of sharing, the sense of common ownership, the sense of joint participation, which were once at the very root of the idea of socialism, might begin to have some reality once more. And here too the real grass-roots are one degree lower still. Even *within* each enterprise, some decisions can be reached jointly in the individual workshop or shop-floor, by those directly involved. As in parts of Swedish industry today, the maximum autonomy and independence can be given, even within an integrated factory, to an individual group of workers, given their own production targets, to be reached by whatever methods they themselves decide, perhaps practising a form of socialism among themselves. Craft workshops can more easily share control.

Finally, equally far down in the grass-roots, in the school, the community centre, the housing estate, there is scope for autonomy, for individual, shared decision-making. In the school, parents, teachers, and even older pupils, can join together in running the establishment, according to the methods and principles they themselves have jointly decided; with far greater freedom in the choice of curriculum and of disciplinary methods, far less controlled by the rules and regulations laid down by local and national authorities, than is the case today. In the housing estate, whether public or private, the residents could be given authority to reach decisions together, within a set annual budget, concerning amenities and improvements and common undertakings, at little additional cost (but here again scale is important – decisions for a council estate of 5000 people will evoke far less sense of participation and far less interest than decisions reached in each street, or in an individual block of flats). Finally, in the community centre, providing it serves a genuine community, a living neighbourhood, as does a village hall, rather than a vast and amorphous borough, joint decisions can be reached about many genuinely local affairs, community activities, youth clubs, recreation, welfare services, so long as councils at a higher level are prepared to relinquish some of their existing powers. So long as genuinely local bodies are allowed to consider nothing but footpaths and graveyards it is scarcely surprising if interest flags.

The goal of 'participation', so much discussed in recent years, depends totally on a breaking-down into units of this kind. Where large numbers are involved, decision-making cannot be truly shared. At a meeting of many hundreds, few have the opportunity to speak, and they will not necessarily be representative. Even in purely mathematical terms, a share of a twenty-thousandth in a decision is clearly worth less than a share of a hundredth or of a tenth. Only if decisions are taken at a genuinely local level, genuinely at the grass-roots, therefore, can the goal of social participation, social control, and social ownership have much meaning.

Only if a sense of belonging can once more be mobilised, only if

ordinary men and women can be given the opportunity to control
their own lives by sharing in decision-making, only therefore at the
genuinely grass-roots level, can the ideals of socialism today be
adequately realised, and the sense of community that has largely
disappeared from modern societies be once more revived.

9.4 *The Revival of Diversity*

Equally important with the rediscovery of community is the
revival of diversity: the reawakening of the variety and differences
within mankind which the centralising force of modern society has
tended to stifle.

To some extent the revival of the community, of small-scale units
of organisation, will automatically have this effect. The more the
local unit, the individual enterprise, housing estate or school can
organise its own affairs in its own way, the more they will gradually
come to diverge: in the policies they favour, in the patterns of
existence they provide, the value-system each seeks to express. If
the downward-moving forces from the top, the demands of organisation, which are the main standardising influences at the present
time, can be gradually reduced, the scope and freedom for greater
diversity will to some extent be automatically enhanced.

But here too there will be needed a *conscious* effort to stimulate
that process, the *deliberate* encouragement of diversity, if the
standardising forces of modern mass communications are to be
counteracted. The existence of mass media can scarcely be undone,
any more than the existence of better communications of other
kinds. There can however be deliberate effort to promote diversity
among those media: to make available the widest possible choice of
content and editorial policy among newspapers, of programme-
content in television programmes, of the style and character of
plays and films on show. But this can be achieved only if there is
some resistance to the almost irresistible: to the overwhelming and
standardising influence of the box-office, the desire to attract the
largest possible number of viewers, readers, or cinema-goers, and
so to reproduce endless marginal variations on the lowest common
multiple of popular taste.

At present the trend in these fields is in the opposite direction. In
most countries the number of newspapers is declining. The

readership of those remaining is increasing and competition between them intensifying. Their dependence on advertising revenue, and the pursuit of ever larger circulations for advertisers, further promotes the trend towards increasing sameness. Each must publish precisely the same stories about the same scandals concerning the same celebrities, the same conventional centre-right political attitudes, the same number of nude photographs, if they are to be able to compete. For the same reason, however many different television channels may exist, they are obliged under a commercial or competitive system to show precisely similar programmes, the same comedians, pop-groups and variety shows, the same quiz programmes and party-games, in precisely similar proportions: because only this will retain the mass audience.

The result is that, though each programme possibly appeals to more people than any alternative might, virtually no group or individual is satisfied. For everybody belongs to a minority of one kind or another, and no minorities of any kind are satisfied by programmes that are exclusively directed to the majority. The majority can only be fully satisfied, therefore, by greater not less, diversity, by more attention devoted to appealing to minority tastes. Entire pages, or entire newspapers, could be given to presenting the type of material and discussion which appeals to readers numbered in hundreds or even tens of thousands, instead of only in millions as today. Minority groups could be invited to produce their own programmes, or write their own columns. And governments and other authorities could provide subsidies that would enable such a variety of tastes to be adequately catered for. Public support could be given to television channels designed to provide for minority rather than majority audiences, for example by covering many or all of the overheads.[1] Governments might spread advertising among the widest possible range of journals and newspapers. They could give adequate subsidies for the operation of radio and television stations to ensure that more adequate time is given to serious discussion of controversial topics, and to the expression of minority views. Libraries, public and private, could support minority journals which might otherwise be unable to survive.

Another important way of promoting diversity is by assisting, encouraging and even promoting voluntary associations for those with particular interests or to promote particular causes. These may provide alternative channels for the expression of views, to counterbalance, or to influence, those expressed by more powerful organisations, political parties and other bodies. They may keep alive causes and creeds that might otherwise die. Community associations and clubs and societies may sustain interests and activities the individual alone could not maintain. Local authorities may help such associations, for example by subsidising the activities of minority groups, and providing facilities for them in community centres. Voluntary associations may then provide some counterweight to the official organisations which otherwise dominate most areas of life today.

Perhaps even more important, if the standardising influences are to be overcome, is the need for more diversity in education. For it is here above all that basically similar methods of instruction in similar types of school by similarly trained teachers is in danger of instilling a nationwide uniformity of knowledge, belief and attitude. Teachers themselves may not wish this. They may consciously stress creativity and originality in their work. But in practice the pressures of supervision and inspection, national qualifications both for teachers and pupils, national examinations and national syllabuses, make it almost impossible for any worthwhile degree of variety, either in subject-matter or method, to be introduced. The pressure to establish exact equality in education has the same effect. In consequence the school runs the risk of becoming a sausage-machine, producing ever-increasing numbers of products that are uniformly well-stuffed, but also equally undistinguished (in the exact sense).

Only decentralisation of the control of education will encourage the development of unorthodox methods and syllabuses and so reduce standardisation. We have already suggested that teachers and parents should largely control each school, with the least possible interference from above. The establishment of a wide variety of schools experimenting in their own methods and syllabuses (for example, for the specially religious, the specially athletic, the specially artistic, the specially scientific, the specially academic, the specially mechanical or inventive) could help to create divergent personalities and talents. Parents could choose the type of school suited to their child's special talents; and the headmasters should normally accept all applicants. The need for equality presupposes equal *opportunities* for all in education (which can certainly not be provided through selection to privileged schools at an early age, still less by the *purchase* of educational opportunities for money); but it does not logically presuppose an exactly *similar* education for all, regardless of interests or aptitudes. Indeed to provide identical education for children who by their nature are unlike, to seek to make non-academic children academic, or vice versa, is in itself a form of injustice (as well as of inefficiency).

What needs to be ensured, therefore, is that parents are provided with the maximum possible *choice* of school. This should be limited as little as possible by geographical, and not at all by financial, considerations. While first schools should perhaps remain essentially community schools to which all children of a locality go, and so become a form of community focus, secondary schools should be open to all over a wide area, according to the *style* of education they provide. And local authorities would need to pursue a deliberate policy of encouraging such diversity among them. In this way schools may be chosen increasingly according to the basic values, methods of teaching and subject-matter they favour, rather than according to the age-range, district, or intelligence quotient they cater for. Some would be especially concerned with creativity, some with discipline and self-control, some with inventiveness, some with science, some with music and the arts, and so on.

One of the main reasons why diversity in education has become more important today is the increase in leisure-time in the modern world. In a rational system the greater part of education should be directly designed to equip people for leisure, since this will constitute by far the greater part of their lives. By providing greater knowledge and training in the arts, for example, schools can provide an inexhaustible resource which will last pupils throughout their days. The capacity to draw or to paint, or for handicrafts, a knowledge of flowers and birds, an appreciation of the theatre and cinema, an interest in the history of coins or stamps or motorcars, may serve as a far more important support in future life than a smattering, in precisely equal proportions, and regardless of natural interest, of mathematics, science, geography or scripture is likely to do. Similarly, if consciousness of the leisure revolution had percolated, government investment, government legislation and government activities would be devoted as much or more to providing satisfying and enriching spare-time activities as in providing means of producing more and more commodities people have less and less need or desire to consume. If leisure is to be effectively used, the study and promotion of enjoyment perhaps today needs as much study as that of learning.

The deliberate effort to promote diversity, spontaneity and independence could be made in these ways the primary aim of policy, even at the expense of functional goals. The pursuit of 'growth' at all costs remains a rational political goal for countries in which poverty remains widespread. It is questionable whether, in a world whose natural resources are rapidly being exhausted, it should remain the supreme object of policy for nations that have achieved the prosperity of most modern Western societies; still less that it should occupy their governments and parliaments to the exclusion of virtually all else, as today. The ultimate concern must be the quality of life society can make available to its citizens: not the 'good life', but the good lives, the many different forms of good life that may be chosen by different individuals. And for that end the type of community organisation adopted is far more important than economic growth.

This demands far more thought than hitherto among politicians and political thinkers about the relationship of particular kinds of social or political institution to particular human satisfactions. For though the dangers that men confront from their own political institutions may be greater today than at any previous time, so also are the opportunities they present. The fact that man has now attained self-consciousness in a social as well as an individual sense, transforms his capacities as a political animal. Until today the type of political order men have created has been the effect mainly of the hazard of history, of mutual competition for power, whether individual or collective, of passive inheritance from the past, or of the blind forces of integration and organisation, rather than of conscious *choice* of socially desirable types of political system.

Though all these factors retain some weight, today more than ever men have the opportunity deliberately to choose, or even to *create* the types of order – economic, political, legal and social – which they believe can provide for them the satisfactions they value most highly. More than at any previous time it has become possible for men to free themselves, from the prison of the present and the shackles of the past; to analyse which are those forms of society best equipped to provide particular types of human satisfaction; and to construct the political constitutions and the social institutions required to procure those values most cherished. In this they will need to create both more *diverse* institutions, and more *small-scale* forms of organisation, appropriate to the variety of humankind and human aspirations. Only this will counteract the overwhelming pressures to conformity and uniformity; make possible creative evolution rather than mechanical role-performance. Only this, likewise, will make possible the full achievement of the ideals of socialism, by allowing the individual to build his own community according to his own beliefs; to share, in willing participation and mutual assistance, within a living and organic human community.

10 Socialism in the Stratosphere: World Socialism

10.1

The monopolisation of the concept and ideals of socialism by the state has not only divorced it from any association with a meaningful human community. It also means that it has become increasingly irrelevant to the inequalities that are most important in the modern world.

For years the inequalities with which men were primarily concerned were inevitably those that existed within their own communities, since these were the ones which were most visible: those they saw within the village, town or region within which they dwelt. But within the last century or two the area of visible inequalities widened, and they became concerned above all about those that were visible within their own state. They became aware that the same inequalities that they saw within their own village or town existed in almost exactly similar form in other villages and towns of their nation. Above all they knew that the state alone possessed the machinery through which such inequalities might ultimately be reduced. It was therefore not surprising that for many years socialists everywhere saw socialism as a system which might be used to remedy inequalities within their own *national* community.

Such a conception is no longer possible. This is partly because, as we saw earlier, inequalities between states become far greater than those within states. While at one time there were some rich and some poor, both in each state and in all states, today virtually everybody in the rich states is better off than virtually everybody in the poor states (if not in personal income, at least in the amenities and opportunities which are open to them). But even more, the change has come about because those inequalities are not only greater than those within states; they have become equally visible. Those in Britain are aware of the poverty of those in Bangladesh;

perhaps more significant, those in Bangladesh are aware of the wealth of those in Britain, as much as of those in their own lands.

Once again, one of the fundamental forces of change is the improvement in communications. A century ago, even if *most* people in India were poorer than *most* people in the US, it was possible for the great majority in both countries to ignore that fact. For the vast majority in both countries knew virtually nothing of the other country or the way people lived within it. Today this is no longer true. Virtually all the inhabitants of both know from the cinema, from the television, from the press and from hearsay something at least of the other, and of the standard of living which prevails within it. Thus today not only is the difference in standard of living between the two infinitely greater than a century ago; there is, with modern means of communication, far greater awareness of that difference. Because consciousness has become worldwide, so too has *concern*.

This change, the emergence of an international consciousness, and so an international political consciousness, affects not only the traditional concerns of socialism, but the conceptions of political theory generally. For the simple and most fundamental concern of political philosophy has always been the problem of obligation: what was the nature of the duty, if any, owed by the citizen to the state. If such a duty existed, was it based only on the state's coercive power to exact allegiance; on convenience; on conditioning; on a theoretical 'social contract'; or did it have some ultimate moral justification, related to the duty of the individual to his fellow-men generally? Whichever of these justifications was favoured, all of them, with the possible exception of the first (which is in any case increasingly discredited), are radically affected by the broadening of the boundaries of political consciousness which modern communications have brought about.

If political obligation is based ultimately on convenience, both to the citizen and to the state, it can be argued that, in a narrowing world of puny states having innumerable interests in common, convenience, both for the citizen and the state, is better served by a broad-based sense of obligation to mankind as a whole than it can be by a proliferation of national allegiances. If the sense of obligation is said to be based on the more traditional, but essentially similar, concept of a social contract between citizens, with each other and with the authority set up over them, again it can today be argued that the benefits of such a contract are more

adequately secured, above all in the field of security (to which the
social contract was once especially applied), if it is held to bind
together members of the human race as a whole, and to enjoin on
them a recognition of their obligation to authorities which all
human beings recognise, rather than if it is applied separately
among a proliferation of partial authorities. If obligation is the
effect only of conditioning through the socialising pressures created
by states themselves, then clearly that obligation can have no
absolute power, and could quickly be transformed if the socialising
pressures themselves were changed. Finally, if the obligation to the
state is held to be associated with some moral obligation of the
citizen to his fellow-men generally, then it is still more difficult to
explain why the obligation should suddenly cease at the frontiers of
his own state; why he should be bound by an obligation only to
fellow-men carrying a particular passport, rather than an obligation to mankind as a whole.

In practice such theories of obligation were normally applied to
whatever type of political organisation happened to be in existence at any one time. Thus, so long as the state was the primary
form of political institution, any such theory was used to justify
obligations to the state. As the world today becomes increasingly
an integrated social, and even political, community, theories of
obligation may increasingly be applied to the duty, if any, which
men owe towards the international community within which all
men live.

While this problem of obligation confronts any political theory,
it is a particularly acute one for socialism. Socialists have always
denied that they were nationalists. They have always proclaimed a
noble, if somewhat misty, ideal of international brotherhood, of
'socialist internationalism'. But in practice, because they have
inherited, with little question, the institutions of the state, and the
assumption that this was the basic form of political organisation,
they have failed to put those fine ideals into practice. They have
continued to take for granted that the principles of socialism must
be applied within the framework of the national state.

Today, however, when the inequalities between states are so
manifestly wider than any which exist within states and when it
becomes not totally utopian to conceive of political organisation at
a higher level, that traditional nation-based attitude becomes
increasingly anachronistic. If socialism is concerned about remedying inequalities, and about the social ownership of the means of

production as a means of doing so, it is increasingly international socialism which it must now proclaim.

10.2 *The Framework of World Socialism*

The beginnings of a structure of international government have, far more than is often realised, already come into being.

Over the past century, and especially over the last thirty years, a network of international institutions has been established which could be made, if member governments so wished, the foundations for a system of world administration, and the instrument of world redistribution. The international institutions which receive most public attention are those which are political in character. But because these deal with the subjects on which states are in most bitter conflict, these are inevitably the ones which are least advanced and with goals least integrated. It is above all those whose purposes are purely practical – technical or economic – which have gone furthest in transferring decision-making power from the national to the international level, and are therefore most likely to become the instruments of an effective world government in the future.[1]

The first to be established were those concerned with communications. The first, now over a century old, took responsibility for the running of the world's postal and telegraph systems (the UPU and the ITU). These have been followed more recently by corresponding organisations dealing with air transport and shipping (ICAO and IMCO). Almost as old as the first two is the organisation concerned with meteorology, which today coordinates the meteorological services of all countries of the world, organises a large number of meteorological stations throughout the world, and runs world centres where the information obtained from all these sources is processed (WMO). Though apparently technical, such organisations do in fact, even in their present relatively undeveloped form, bring about a considerable degree of redistribution. Their budgets are financed on a progressive principle, and all have technical assistance programmes for transferring technology in their own field to poorer countries, and also undertake similar programmes with funds provided by the UN development programme. At least they redistribute knowledge.

There are in addition a number of agencies which can be

regarded as embryonic world social services. The World Health
Organisation, which in terms of its budget is the largest of all these
specialised agencies, not only organises a number of *common* services
such as the notification of diseases on a world scale, regulations to
prevent the transmission of diseases, world campaigns against
particular diseases (so virtually eliminating smallpox and ma-
laria, for example), the testing and certification of drugs, coordi-
nating research, world-wide atmospheric sampling, and so on; it
also gives substantial assistance to poor countries in improving their
own medical and public health services. In the field of education,
the United Nations Educational Scientific and Cultural Organisation organises and coordinates world scientific and research
programmes, runs various common services in the field of science,
arranges the protection of well-known monuments and other parts
of the world's cultural heritage, and above all gives large-scale
assistance to poor countries in improving their educational services
and abolishing illiteracy. The International Labour Organisation,
originally concerned with raising standards of government legislation concerning labour conditions all over the world, now has
extensive programmes in the field of industrial training, labour
administration, unemployment policies, and many other forms of
assistance to help poorer countries. The UN itself runs a number of
programmes in this field, designed to provide assistance in the
performance of a number of social objectives, such as the abolition
of the trade in narcotic drugs, the abolition of slavery, improvement of women's rights, the ending of racial discrimination, the
improvement of housing conditions and the reform of penal
administration.

Even more important are the world institutions which have
emerged in the economic field and which now perform a
recognised world role in their own field. For example, the
International Monetary Fund has made itself the authority
responsible for the management of the world's monetary system
and, by its decisions concerning credit, parities, the use of gold, and
above all by the creation of special drawing rights, exercises an
increasingly powerful influence on the running of the world
economy. It too operates various facilities and arrangements which
are designed specifically to assist poor countries, though it has so far
resisted the simplest and most radical way it might help, through
the direct distribution of credit, in the form of SDRs, to poor
countries for the financing of their imports. Similarly in the field of

trade the General Agreement on Tariffs and Trade and the United Nations Conference on Trade and Development exercise an increasing influence on the commercial and commodity policies pursued by national administrations all over the world, and again themselves organise, or persuade governments to administer, trade arrangements which give special benefits to the poorer nations of the world.

Some international institutions have acquired powers relating to various natural resources. The International Atomic Energy Agency exercises an important role in supervising and inspecting the transfer of nuclear materials, in organising safeguards of various kinds for those who work with nuclear materials, undertakes research into new and cheaper forms of nuclear energy, especially those likely to be of benefit to poorer countries, and provides extensive assistance in the field of atomic energy. There is however a strong case for a world agency responsible for energy generally. At present there exist only partial bodies, representing for example the producers and consumers of oil, but no permanent forum for discussing world oil problems, still less for discussing energy questions of other kinds. The same is true of other resources and materials. For a number of individual commodities, there exist international agreements designed to stabilise the trade, and reduce fluctuations in price, all of which require some degree of international management. But there is a case, here too, for some international body or Commission on Natural Resources which would have general responsibility for keeping an eye on behalf of the world community on the supply situation and the rate of depletion for all the major raw materials, which at present are in danger of being exhausted if natural economic forces are permitted to operate entirely unchecked.

The rate of growth of all these bodies, both in terms of their budgets and in terms of the responsibilities placed on them, has been extremely fast over the last two decades. In a world for which national authorities have become far too small to undertake many of the responsibilities they have traditionally performed, authority is increasingly being transferred, almost unnoticed, to a higher level of government. A wide range of common services are now being performed for the world as a whole.

All such agencies bring about some redistribution from rich countries to poor. They are all financed on a progressive basis, with poor countries contributing at a lower rate, and rich countries at a higher rate. Yet their services (even apart from their assistance programmes) benefit all equally. Thus, just as within national states a high level of public expenditure and public services brings about some degree of redistribution, so a high level of expenditure amongst international institutions brings about some redistribution between states. International socialists, therefore, who wish to bring about a more rapid distribution of wealth and welfare from rich to poor in the world as a whole, will wish to see such institutions strengthened, and will wish above all to secure a larger volume of resources for them in the performance of their tasks.

Such bodies, however, are not *specifically* concerned with redistribution. And international socialists who wish to see such a transfer of resources will be still more concerned with those institutions whose primary function it is to bring about a redistribution from rich countries to poor.

10.3 *International Redistribution*

Besides these various world institutions concerned with specific functional tasks there exist a few that are specifically concerned with the transfer of resources from rich to poor.

It is only since 1945 that any institution has existed for this purpose. The League of Nations provided advice and assistance for a few countries suffering financial difficulties (mainly in East Europe). And it organised international discussions of various world economic problems. But the conception of a general obligation among rich countries to provide 'aid' to poor countries emerged primarily in the years after the Second World War. Even then for long the greater part of assistance was provided through bilateral channels, direct from government to government. International bodies for the purpose at first were weak or ineffective. The World Bank (International Bank for Reconstruction and Development), though first set up in 1944, for long was as concerned with the 'reconstruction' of rich countries as with the 'development' of poor ones. And until after 1960 more of its funds had been lent to rich countries than to poor ones.

But meanwhile other institutions had come into being. The UN itself provided, on a small scale, technical assistance to poor countries, both from its regular budget and from voluntary funds for that purpose. A Special Fund devoted to pre-investment projects was

Socialism in the Stratosphere 167

set up, financed by voluntary contributions, and was eventually merged with the UN's technical assistance programme in the United Nations Development Programme. The funds subscribed to this rapidly grew until they now amount to about 500 million dollars a year. The World Bank too founded a special subsidiary, the International Development Association, through which it lent on 'soft' terms (that is, with deferred repayments and at interest rates of only 2%). Between them the World Bank and the International Development Association now lend something over eight billion dollars a year to poor countries. There are also a number of regional development banks, under the auspices of the UN, which lend money to poor countries for development purposes.

These institutions represent a huge advance on anything which has existed in human history before. At least they reflect a dawning recognition that men and governments are subject to an obligation of mutual assistance across national boundaries as well as within them. Their development has helped to evoke an emerging sentiment that men and governments are concerned not only with the development of their own national states, but are engaged together in a common task of developing their common world.

There are however two main deficiencies in these programmes. One is that by far the greater part takes the form of non-concessionary loans at commercial rates of interest. This makes necessary very large repayments, made in scarce foreign exchange, from poor countries to rich. It is indeed doubtful, as we saw in Chapter 8, whether it represents any net transfer of resources at all. Only grants and loans made on concessionary terms can therefore be regarded as assistance in the proper sense. Secondly, the programmes, even including loans at commercial rates, are tiny in scale. Most governments in rich countries have so far found it impossible even to reach the relatively modest goal of spending 0.75% of national income on such assistance: at present the figure is on average around half that small percentage for the rich countries as a whole.

There is still another, and more important, reason why such programmes cannot begin to represent anything which could be regarded as a form of world socialism: a recognised obligation to transfer from rich to poor on a world scale, with machinery to bring this about. At present the payments made are purely voluntary, at the discretion of the givers. They are about as close to socialism, therefore, as the voluntary donations of the wealthier classes to charity in Victorian Britain. For anything that could begin to deserve the name of world socialism, there would need to be some mechanism which provided for *automatic* redistribution from rich to poor, comparable to that brought about among individuals through the tax system and socialisation of property within states.

Since there exists no world government, still less a world system of taxation, such a form of international redistribution is still a long way off. It is, however, just possible to sketch the kind of scenario which might lead to something not altogether different.

In the first place, the pressures on rich countries to give could be intensified. Instead of merely waiting on unilateral decisions by each government, new institutions for considering such matters might be established. An international committee, in which all the main donor and recipient governments were represented, might consider world development needs on a continuing basis. It would fix every year a target, in absolute terms, for the total transfer of resources aimed at, and criteria for deciding the proportion to be contributed by each donor. It might then institute negotiations with each individual donor government to secure from it the proportion allocated to it in each year. That proportion could be adjusted from year to year, according to the circumstances, the balance of payments position, the rate of economic growth and other factors affecting each government. But the level finally fixed would be determined by the international committee and not by the donor government itself. That government would then be called on to justify publicly any failure to meet that obligation. The pressures could develop in intensity. Eventually governments might be expected to be as reliable in paying contributions for this purpose as they have become in paying their contributions to the budgets of international organisations (for which there has been no defaulting by any government over the past thirty years).

A system on these lines, under which the payment of development assistance became eventually virtually automatic for each government, would represent a substantial advance on anything which exists today. It would, however, represent a system more comparable to progressive taxation, as applied by conservative governments as well as socialist within the state, than to a form of socialism. Socialism in the proper sense demands some redistribution of ownership as well as of income.

Here too it is possible to see small steps which might eventually

lead in that direction. The principle of 'participation' - the transfer
of a share at least in the control of undertakings based in the territory of another state to the government of that state (so far used almost entirely in relation to the ownership of oil production)—could
begin to be more widely applied. It could come to be more widely
accepted that industrial undertakings of all kinds at present under
the ownership of foreign companies should be progressively (and if
possible voluntarily) transferred to the governments or nationals of
the host state, as has occurred in the case of oil. Eventually a
situation might be reached in which the greater part of the
industries and enterprises that were formerly foreign-owned fell
into the hands of the host state. In this case there would come about
some transfer of property as well as of income from rich states to
poor.

But, as we have seen, industrial investment is in any case today
increasingly concentrated in the home state rather than abroad;
and a system under which the resources and industrial property of
each country was domestically owned would not in itself necessarily bring about a much more equal world. For anything in the
nature of 'socialism' at the international level, something more
than this would be required; the acquisition of certain resources
and undertakings by the international community, to be run in the
interests of the inhabitants of all states, and therefore used as a
means of redistribution.

There is already at least one area where this may come about
within the near future. This is in the case of the resources of the
international seabed in the area beyond national jurisdiction (that
is in the area beyond each state's own continental shelf or economic
zone). During the international discussions on this subject over the
last ten years, one principle which has been fairly widely agreed is
that these resources are the 'common heritage of mankind', and
should be jointly administered by an international body. It is
widely accepted that the exploitation of such resources would be
undertaken only with the authority of the international body,
would occur only in return for royalties paid to the international
authority which would be used for redistribution to poorer states,
or would be undertaken by an international body for the purpose,
whose profits would be similarly redistributed among all states.

Such a system would indeed represent a form of world socialism.
The resources concerned would be commonly owned, and the
benefit from their exploitation would be shared among the world

community as a whole on the basis of needs (in other words the poorest countries and their inhabitants would receive the largest benefit). In other words, exactly the same system employed within socialist states or by socialist institutions within states, under which resources are publicly owned and managed in the interest of the community as a whole, would now be applied at the world level; and public resources would be publicly managed in the interest of the world community as a whole.

Once established in that instance, there is no reason why eventually the same principle should not be applied in other cases. Where new resources were found, in the Antarctic or in heavenly bodies, for example, where new undertakings were established, such as new international communications facilities (the world communications satellite system (INTELSAT) is an example), they could be jointly, that is internationally, owned, and the benefits shared among all nations according to need. Eventually such a system might be applied to existing resources as well. That system would for the first time implement on an international basis, that is in the only true and full sense, the old socialist principle: from each according to his ability, to each according to his needs. The social ownership of international resources would be used to bring about an international redistribution of benefits, just as the social ownership of national resources has for long been used to bring about the redistribution of benefits within states.

10.4 *International Equality and International Diversity*

Thus a philosophy of world socialism would be designed to bring about a greater measure of equality between states, just as traditional socialism, that is, state socialism, has been designed to bring a greater measure of equality within them.

The emergence of a single world community changes many of the problems surrounding equality. The capacity of any single society or state to establish a more equal distribution of income and opportunities is now conditioned by what takes place in other societies. For example, so long as certain kinds of talent receive a high level of reward in one society, no others can afford to allow their own rewards for the same talents to fall too far below that level; for they may otherwise suffer a drain of brains, of skills and expertise of every kind to those areas where they receive the highest reward. Just as Britain and other European countries risk losing trained scientists, engineers, doctors and others to the US, Asia and Latin American countries may lose them to Europe, and the least developed countries of all to those that are one stage ahead. As a result of that process, inequalities in economic performance and standard of living may be still further intensified. Certainly equalisation will be halted. In a single integrated international political community, equality becomes indivisible.

The reduction of inequalities in income and in wealth becomes, therefore, a problem which no individual state can any longer tackle in isolation; it is a problem for the international community as a whole. Judgements of what differentials represent suitable incentives, or suitable rewards for responsibility, skill or hardship, can no longer be considered in isolation, for they are affected by the differentials paid in other neighbouring societies. Inequalities between individuals performing precisely similar functions in different states become increasingly difficult to justify convincingly. They can of course be *explained*: on the basis of different states' productive capacity, for example. But such arguments would never be used to justify differences in income within states: nobody seeks, in determining the income to be paid to a doctor or a teacher or a miner, to calculate exactly the income of the region in which they work. Again, if wide differences in educational opportunity are regarded as unjustified within states, can such differences be any more justified between nations?

The traditional use of different criteria in considering inequalities between states results not from a sudden difference in principle at the international level, but from the narrow political consciousness which the all-powerful 'state' has created, and the apparent lack of a suitable mechanism for redistribution between states. Yet there does exist already in embryo, as we have just seen, precisely such a mechanism. There are levies by the international community, comparable to taxation within states: payments made by governments to a number of international agencies and bodies, at varying rates according to means. There exist, though only on a tiny scale, a number of services, comparable to the common services provided by governments for citizens. And there is direct assistance to poor nations, comparable to welfare services within states, through international institutions for the purpose.

In its method of assessment, this redistribution is probably quite as progressive as anything that takes place within states. The standard form of assessment, used in almost all UN agencies, is based primarily on national income. The effect is that the US alone pays a quarter of the total budget of most organisations, while half the budgets are provided by the half-dozen most developed countries alone. But the crucial point affecting redistribution is not the degree of progressiveness, but the *scale* of the budgets, and so of the programmes that result. That scale is tiny at present. Thus while the US contribution represents a large proportion of the UN budget, it is a totally insignificant proportion of her own national income. It is insignificant even in relation to the developing nations' income. The result is that the disequalisation that takes place through differing rates of growth a head, and the different base from which growth takes place, is at present far greater than the equalisation through redistribution by international agencies.

As these mechanisms for redistribution develop, as consciousness of standards of living elsewhere becomes more acute, as more and more individuals have direct first-hand experience of the way of life of other countries having a totally different standard of living, it may be that the conception of world socialism here outlined will cease to be so outlandish as it may appear today. And it will come increasingly to be recognised that the sense of mutual obligation which that concept embodies, a mutual obligation which does not halt abruptly and arbitrarily at the nearest national frontier, corresponds far better with the ethical philosophies commonly held today than the conceptions of national or state socialism (and indeed other political philosophies) under which obligation is discriminatory not general, partial rather than universal. For at its root socialism represents above all a concern for fellow-men. And there is no clearly discernible reason why it should refer only to those fellow-men who happen to salute the same national flag.

But the second effect of a genuinely international political consciousness is that political thought and political action no longer need to be concerned only with the values and institutions of a single, ideal state, valid for all alike. It becomes possible to conceive of alternative states, practising alternative political philosophies and expressing alternative political values. For the first time political *choice* becomes available. The citizen is no longer assumed to inherit automatically the state in which he is born, and to be inevitably committed to that state which, if he wishes to realise his own political beliefs and ideals, must be changed accordingly. On the contrary the search would be for those varying forms of political institution and political society which would correspond to the *varying* dispositions and values of each individual citizen. And the corollary of accepting a form of obligation that is universal - to all fellow-men elsewhere - is not the demand to create a single universal world state practising a majority creed, but the recognition of the right of each citizen to choose his *own* political institutions and his own state, a recognition in other words of the demands of diversity, of the need for many small-scale political communities (of the type we considered in the last chapter), so that the widest possible choice is available.

For today it is possible for people to express their political desires, not by altering the political institutions or their own community or state, but by transferring themselves to that state or community which best accords with their own political values and ideals. In theory some choice has always been available. It has nearly always been possible to travel from one state to the next, and often to settle there. But in practice the barriers of language and culture, of tradition and inconvenience, not to speak of immigration and citizenship regulations, have been so large as to be almost insurmountable. Today personal mobility creates political mobility.

This marks a huge change for political theory. When people can move comparatively easily from one state to another, when loyalties are less firmly rooted to the state of birth, traditional concerns - about obligation, freedom, the rights and duties of citizens to governments and vice versa - become less relevant. The traditional attempt to devise the one perfect state, where the good life is available for all and 'justice' finally secured, where a political ideology valid for all peoples and all countries is put into practice, becomes irrelevant and nonsensical. In such circumstances the concern need not be to create the single ideal state, catering equally for all; but to create a multiplicity of ideal states, ideal constitutions and ideal ideologies, each suited to the variety of temperaments, beliefs and value-systems which may prevail among mankind as a whole.

Political thought then becomes concerned to discover what is the relationship between particular values, demands and tempera-ments and particular types of political organisation and structure. Value questions have in recent years been regarded as scarcely respectable subjects of political study, because beyond the realm of political 'science'. Yet in former times political philosophy was largely devoted to considering precisely such questions. Many political writings were indeed in effect descriptions of the types of state that would satisfy the system of values upheld by the author himself and his first concern was to define those values. But for them it was taken for granted, and implicit in this aim, that there could be only one such state. The possibility of a choice between states, each expressing a different set of values, never appeared to be available.

Today therefore theory becomes in a sense a study of alternative Utopias. Which types of society can best fulfil particular aims and ideals? What is the sacrifice that must be made, in attaining one value, of others, perhaps almost equally cherished? What social and psychological values might be attained if the object of economic growth as the supreme goal of governments was abandoned? If complete material equality was made the supreme end, what would be the cost in other respects? If central government was reduced to the barest minimum, and all else left to local authorities, what would be the implications? If money was abolished, what would happen elsewhere in the system? If all secrecy in government was done away with, what would be the sacrifice in boldness of decision-making? If all major questions were determined by referenda, what would be the loss in efficiency? What, in other words, are the implications of one choice for other possibilities?

For this a more intensive examination of some of the pioneering communities of the last two centuries, their problems and their achievements might be valuable. If it is true, as some studies suggest, that those have been less successful, and have lasted less long, in the twentieth century than in the nineteenth, what are the reasons? Is this a manifestation of the all-powerful pressures of conformity and consensus at the national level? What is the essential condition to be fulfilled for the successful establishment of self-sufficient communities of this type, devoted to the fulfilment of a particular ideal and way of life? And what kind of relationship is possible for them with governments within the outside world?[2]

It is only when there exist different types of community practising different social, political and cultural systems, with free movement between them, that the ultimate ideal of so many political theorists, a harmony between the purposes, values and aspirations of the individual and that of the political community he belongs to, begins to be attainable. Neither the forcible conformity imposed by absolute governments, such as has been seen in the past, nor the conditioning by pressures of public opinion so that the citizen is 'forced to be free', as is often imposed today, achieves that end. For each may involve, by different methods, the subordinaton of the individual to social purposes and values which he has no effective opportunity to influence or reject. Since individuals have varying temperaments, and opinions, and varying views of how a state should be managed, no single state can provide equal satisfaction for all. Though men may share a large number of satisfactions in common, they will interpret each in different ways, and demand them in different balances. And the forms of political organisation that might best afford desired goals to some may deny to others those they value most dearly of all. True choice among political values and political systems therefore can be achieved only by a choice *among* states and communities.

Thus only a variety of states and communities, and the maximum choice among them, can provide the freedom, the sense of self-direction, the absence of constraint or unwanted obligation, which political philosophy has traditionally sought. This obviously demands a broad equality, or at least compatibility, in living standards: otherwise all would go where living standards are highest. But in other respects the greater the diversity the greater the aggregate satisfaction of values. This demands a central authority as flexible and invisible as possible; exerted rather through agreed norms of interaction than through the overt exercise of power. Only sufficient *consciousness* of the needs of diversity, and of the dangers of excessive uniformity, might achieve this, by countering the pressures for ever-increasing power at the centre. Under these conditions the state, in which authority has been concentrated for so long, may at last relinquish some of the authority and loyalty that it has monopolised, both upwards to international institutions above, and downwards to local institutions below.

Man's supreme superiority over other animals is his capacity to construct his own social institutions, according to his own purposes and values. But while man as a race can construct those institutions, man as an individual cannot. Only the availability of many different types of structure can provide for individuals the opportunity to choose the political structure that most nearly satisfies his own values and desires. And only in small-scale communities where every member can participate in essential decisions, and where social ownership need not presuppose a remote and inflexible leviathan, can he enjoy full control over, and so freedom within, his own political existence.

In this way the inexorable centralising and standardising pressures of organisation might at last be counteracted by the vitalising forces of diversity and change. And the age-old ideals of socialism, the sharing of resources and activity on a basis of equality, could be achieved not through remote and impersonal authorities beyond the influence of individuals, but within the living communities which have the most real meaning to men and women everywhere.

Notes

INTRODUCTION
1. For a brilliant analysis of this ambivalence of Marx and Engels towards the role of the state see G. Tarschys, *Beyond the State* (Stockholm, 1972).

CHAPTER 1
1. For example by Max Weber.
2. As suggested in F. Tonnies, *Society and Community* (English translation, London, 1955).
3. The Communist parties of Italy and France have made themselves an exception only when converting themselves into social democratic parties proposing few radical changes.

CHAPTER 2
1. S. M. Lipset and R. Bendix, *Social Mobility in Industrial Society* (London, 1959) pp.33-8.
2. Ibid., pp.17-33.

CHAPTER 3
1. K. Marx, *Economic and Philosophical Manuscripts of 1844* (Moscow, 1959) p.124.
2. For further discussion see Chapter 6.

CHAPTER 4
1. David Riesman's *The Lonely Crowd* (New York, 1950) remains one of the best studies of the pressures to conformity in modern societies.

CHAPTER 5
1. J. Locke, *Second Treatise on Government* (1690) 2, 4.
2. W. Sumner, *What Social Classes are to Each Other* (New York, 1883).
3. K. Marx, *Critique of the Gotha Programme* (English translation, London, 1943).
4. K. Marx, *Private Property and Communism* (English translation, London, 1975).
5. J. Locke, *Second Treatise on Government*.
6. J.-J. Rousseau, *Discourse on the Origin of Inequality* (1754).
7. J. S. Mill, *Dissertations and Discussions* (1859) II.
8. For a description of these widely varying benefits see R. M. Titmuss, *Income and Social Change* (London, 1962).
9. Given this total immutability of pay-differentials under 'free collective bargaining', the capacity of the wealthy to evade or avoid taxation aimed at redistribution, and the increasing proportion of taxation levied indirectly, the only means of securing a long-term and irreversible shift in incomes to create a

more equal society is in modern conditions likely to be through a statutory incomes policy designed to secure the fairer distribution of income desired by society (a fact which makes it surprising that many who profess to be socialists in Britain consistently oppose any such radical measure, apparently preferring the law of the jungle which already exists).

10. The differential changes of acquittal or of winning a civil suit in modern societies, at least in the Anglo-Saxon world, according to the differential skill of the advocates are magnified by the entire system applied. A legal system such as our own, based on confrontation and challenge followed by a vote, while perhaps suitable in the conditions of the Middle Ages, is totally inappropriate to a modern society, providing enormous room for faulty decisions according to the variation in the investigating powers, as well as the forensic skill, of the lawyers employed on either side. It places immense responsibility on both judge and jury for reaching a decision of overwhelming importance on the basis of evidence presented in the most partisan, incoherent and confusing form possible – a confusion deliberately fostered by each advocate in relation to all evidence unfavourable to them. A system of initial impartial inquiry by magistrates, with the assistance of the police, and subsequently open to challenge in the lawcourt, as in the continental system, would appear more likely to arrive at objective and fair decisions, and could certainly present the evidence in a more lucid and comprehensive form than the hit-or-miss system at present employed in Britain and the US.

CHAPTER 6

1. This type of argument is found in C. D. Burns, *Democracy* (London, 1935) pp.68–75; H. J. Laski, *A Grammar of Politics* (London, 1925) p.17; H. J. Ford, *Representative Government* (London, 1925) pp.307–9. It was of course Lord Acton who said that 'power corrupts: absolute power corrupts absolutely.'

2. Cf. H. R. G. Greaves, *Foundations of Political Theory* (London, 1958) pp.199ff.; J. R. Pennock, *Liberal Democracy* (New York, 1950) pp.105–15.

3. James Mill, *An Essay on Government* (London, 1821): H. B. Mayo, *An Introduction to Democratic Theory* (Oxford, 1960) p.118; J. Plamenatz, *Men and Society* (London, 1963) pp.30–6.

4. Mayo, op. cit., pp.218–22; N. Riermer, *The Revival of Democratic Theory* (New York, 1962) pp.99–134.

5. R. A. Dahl, *A Preface to Democratic Theory* (Chicago, 1956) pp.132–5; G. C. Field, *Political Theory* (London, 1956) p.124; Mayo, op.cit., pp.219–20.

6. A. D. Lindsay, *The Essentials of Democracy* (Oxford, 1935) pp.78–82; Mayo op.cit., p.75; Sir E. Barker, *Principles of Social and Political Theory* (Oxford, 1951) pp.294–7.

7. Dahl, op. cit., pp.136–7; Riermer, op. cit., p.109.

8. Field, op.cit., pp.123–5; Greaves, op.cit., p.204; H. J. Laski, *An Introduction to Politics* (London, 1931) p.48.

9. The point of decision in practice moves progressively further back into more obscure recesses: from parliament to cabinet; from cabinet to cabinet committee; from there to official committee; finally to the bureaucracy within a department.

10. The decision on wording might perhaps be made by some permanent all-party or non-party body, perhaps judicial, or under the authority of the Speaker of the House of Commons.

11. There might be a system for the registration of organisations 'accredited' to a ministry and normally consulted on matters affecting them. Each ministry would publish immediately the fact that an interest group had approached it (though the content of such representations would of course be confidential). Removal of secrecy *within* pressure-groups may be almost as important: the formulation of policy in private sometimes has the effect that an active minority takes it on a course not necessarily approved by the passive majority of the membership.

12. The Association of Municipal Corporations in Britain for some time demanded the establishment of local urban parish councils within the county borough or municipal borough.

CHAPTER 7

1. Marx, *Economic and Philosophical Manuscripts*.

2. The functioning of this firm is very fully documented, thanks to the writings of those associated with it. See Jacques Elliot, *Changing Culture of a Factory* (London, 1951) and *Glacier Project Papers* (London, 1965); and W. Brown, *Exploration in Management* (London, 1960).

3. For a study of this partnership see A. Flanders and others, *Experiment in Industrial Democracy* (London, 1968); and J. Spedan Lewis, *Partnership for All* (London, 1948) and *Fairer Shares* (London, 1954).

4. For a description of this system see F. Singleton and A. Topham, *Workers' Control in Yugoslavia* (Fabian Society, 1963).

5. For consideration of some of these problems see H. A. Clegg, *A New Approach to Industrial Democracy* (London, 1963).

CHAPTER 8

1. Titmuss, op. cit., p.112.

2. One calculation is that if all pre-tax undistributed income had been included in income there would have been no levelling in personal income between 1939 and 1945, when most of the levelling of the past thirty years in Britain occurred. Between 1949 and 1959 the yearly total of undistributed income of all private companies rose from £914 million to £2147 million, or by 135 per cent (ibid., p.113).

3. *Report of the* [Radcliffe] *Committee on the Working of the Monetary System*, para.450.

4. R. P. Good, *The Individual Income Tax* (Washington, 1966).

5. Gifts among the living have been subject to tax in the US for many years. The capital transfer tax in Britain now secures some of these objects.

6. In the US in recent times less than 10 per cent of new investment is financed by new issues: the rest comes from internal savings or bank loans. In West Germany and Japan the proportion raised on the market is even less.

7. The occasional rise of 'super-competitive' states with no benefit from oil, such as South Korea and Taiwan, is no real exception since even these can compete only in relatively low-technology industries.

CHAPTER 9

1. The simplest method by which governments could assure the survival and independence of newspapers would be by preventing advertising on television (as already done in many countries and recommended for Britain in the Pilkington

Report) or at the very least taxing it more heavily, and so providing more such revenue for newspapers. This would also serve to restore quality to television programmes.

CHAPTER 10

1. For a fuller examination of these organisations and the way their authority might be strengthened see E. Luard, *International Agencies: the Emerging Framework of Interdependence* (London, 1976).

2. For studies of American and British communities of this type over the last two centuries see M. Holloway, *Heaven on Earth* (1951), and W. H. C. Armytage, *Heavens Below* (1965).

Index